THE ANIMAL WORLD

OF

ALBERT SCHWEITZER

Also edited by Charles R. Joy

The Spiritual Life

Selected Writings of Albert Schweitzer

The Animal World of

Albert Schweitzer

Jungle Insights into Reverence for Life

Translated and edited, with an introduction, by

CHARLES R. JOY

Illustrated with drawings by Richard Bartlett
and photographs by Charles R. Joy

THE ECCO PRESS

THE ECCO PRESS
100 West Broad Street
Hopewell, New Jersey 08525
Published simultaneously in Canada by
Penguin Books Canada Ltd., Ontario
Printed in the United States of America
This edition published by arrangement with The Beacon Press

9 8 7 6 5 4 3 2 1

FIRST ECCO EDITION

TO

MONSIEUR LE PÉLICAN

FAITHFUL GUARDIAN

OF

ALBERT SCHWEITZER

Monsieur le Pélican is, like the Doctor, a preacher. On the veranda of the Doctor's house he takes his place, and makes an oration, gesturing vigorously with his wings, and making harsh, throaty noises as he opens his bill wide. He, too, has a mind of his own, and a message to the world.

Contents

Introduction

If Albert Schweitzer were to follow the inclinations of his own heart, his autobiography would appear in two parallel columns: in the first he would tell of books and people, of music and ideas; in the second he would tell of animal friends he has known and loved. Some of the material for such an autobiography now exists at Lambarene in the diary where Schweitzer records the important events of his life. He once showed me a page of it where he had noted two significant arrivals at the hospital on the same day — the Dutch nurse, Maria Lagendijk, and the little, frightened antelope Léonie. It was no disparagement of the work of one of Lambarene's most competent and devoted nurses that the doctor seemed to think one arrival as worthy of notation as the other.

The natives had dug a deep pit on one of the jungle trails to trap animals, and into it plunged an antelope with her small fawn. When the natives arrived, the mother in her terror gave a mighty bound and escaped. The little fawn was left behind. The natives, knowing Doctor Schweitzer's custom of liberally rewarding those who bring him for his care the helpless creatures of the forest, animals hurt in some way, or babies whose mothers have been killed, carried the tiny fawn to him. He nursed it on a bottle, kept it in a pen adjoining his study, let it roam about his table in the evening until it began to eat his manuscripts and nibble holes in his trousers. Every afternoon when he had leisure he took it out for a gambol around him on the river bank beneath the palm trees. He would often sit on a low wall beside his house and let Léonie lick his arm for the salt in the perspiration.

"If Léonie licks my arm well, I know I have done a hard day's work," he used to say.

Dr. Schweitzer's relations with the animal life about him are

11

of a very intimate kind. It is not simply that he has a way with him, so that the wild creatures of the jungle often eat from his hand, or permit him to caress them freely. It is more than that. He feels a close tie of kinship with them; together they share the strange and marvelous gift of life. Their life is doubtless as significant to them as his life is to him. They have the same right to consideration, respect and, where possible, affection.

At Edinburgh, when he was delivering the Gifford lectures, he met Sir Wilfred Grenfell of the Labrador Mission and wrote in a guest book: "The hippopotamus is happy to meet the polar bear." The words were written by a man who once expressed a hope that a hippopotamus, disporting in the river before the Lambarene hospital and attacking the dugouts along the shore, might be warned by some premonition to take itself off and so escape the death sentence that otherwise would have to be pronounced against it.

Asked at a meeting where he was about to speak how he should be introduced, Schweitzer replied: "Oh, tell them that this fellow over there who looks like a shaggy dog is Albert Schweitzer."

The pleasantry was uttered by a man who has almost always had dogs around him, and who would not consider it an insult to be likened to a dog. When Mrs. C. E. B. Russell, one of his gifted translators, visited him in Africa and was put in charge of a gang of workmen, she asked Schweitzer how she was to discharge her responsibilities.

"That's very simple," he said, "just imagine yourself a shepherd dog with a flock of sheep, and act accordingly. Then everything will be all right."

Dr. Schweitzer wrote some time ago, asking to see my translation of something he had written in German, in order that he might be quite sure it expressed his thought exactly.

"You know," he said, "I am a timid person, even though it does not appear so. So make allowances for the kinship of my soul with that of my antelopes."

I was writing at my table in Lambarene one day, when Dr. Schweitzer knocked at my door and asked if he might come in. He sat down on the edge of the bed and began to chat. In the midst of the conversation he suddenly got up and, taking a tumbler from the shelf and a blotter from the table, went to the large screened

There are always antelopes in the hospital, and often one or two of them, when small, are permitted to live in the Doctor's rooms, roaming around freely and nibbling at the Doctor's trousers and manuscripts. Here are Léonie and Théodore. They are licking the Doctor's arm for the salt in the perspiration.

window. There, placing the tumbler over a bee that was vainly trying to escape, and carefully sliding the blotter over the top of the
tumbler, he caught the frantic insect, walked to the door, opened
it, and let the bee wing its way to freedom.

Then I remembered that Schweitzer's first teacher in his Alsatian
home had been a bee.

Every country boy learns to know animals — and Albert Schweitzer was a country boy. There were the many farm animals around
him: the horses and the cows the goats, the sheep, the pigs. In the
summer, the cows had to be taken up to the high alps for their
pasturage and, in the fall, brought down again to the sheltered
valleys. Often, the goats were taken down to feed along the banks
of the little river Fecht. To herd the cows and the other animals
was a pleasant occupation, an initiation into the magic enchant-
ment of nature. It gave a boy time for dreams and the "long, long
thoughts of youth." It is not strange that this boy's earliest ambition
was to be a swineherd.

In the dense forests of the uplands, there were wild animals also.
The wild boar and the deer did much damage to the vegetable gardens and, particularly, to the vineyards that climbed the steep hill-
sides to the edge of the evergreens. As late as 1890 wolves roamed
the Munster valley. The fields and forests were alive with birds,
which filled the air with their gay melodies. Almost every little
town had on some tall steeple or chimney its huge stork's nest, to
which every year the storks returned to raise their brood of long-
legged fledglings.

Then there was always a dog around the presbytery to be taken
for romps in the fields or harnessed to a little cart for the delight
of the two boys in the family. Whether it was Phylax, or Sultan,
or another, the dog became a beloved member of the family and
Albert's inseparable companion.

One of the more recent physicians at the Lambarene hospital
remembers his first meeting with Dr. Schweitzer because of his
big black dog. Sultan, the great Newfoundland, was sacrificed on
the African altar: Dr. Schweitzer decided to take him to the new
post of service, but the old dog could not stand the journey and
died before reaching the Ogowe.

An amusing story is told which illustrates the close bond between Schweitzer and these animal friends. Schweitzer, then a teacher of theology at the University of Strassburg, went to call with two other professors of theology on Pastor Klein, an old family friend at Diemeringen. Pastor Klein had a dog of which Doctor Schweitzer was very fond. At tea time, the pastor, taking three lumps of sugar from the table, offered one to the dog, saying, "This piece is from Doctor Novack." The dog turned his head away. "This piece is from Professor Lobstein." Again the dog turned his head away. "This piece is from Doctor Schweitzer." The dog gobbled it down.

Returning from long absences in Africa, Doctor Schweitzer would often surprise his Strassburg friends by remembering the names of their dogs.

Western Europe is a man's continent, but Africa with its jungles has always been an animal's continent, where man is an intruder. Herds of rampaging elephants often lay waste the native villages. No Negro dares venture into the deep forests where "gorilla towns" are known to exist. The hippopotamus and the crocodile rule the rivers. No one travels in the jungle by night; and even by day the narrow, lonely trails are fraught with peril.

Trader Horn, whose trading post was close to where the Lambarene hospital now stands, tells of the early days: "The Ogowe was full of strange life and sounds at early dawn, in fact was a veritable zoo let loose. Hippos would scurry from the papyrus swamps into the deep waters, crocodiles would slide from the banks . . . birds of all descriptions flitted to and fro. Now the beautiful crested crane would rise and fly away, and kingfishers of all kinds, disturbed, would follow them . . . the most beautiful bird in the world, the pippio . . . one mass of green and gold . . . butterflies of all colors and shapes. Sitting perched on the outstretched branches of a large tree . . . several great owls, . . . very tall and . . . motionless with their large, yellow, round eyes fully opened, looking vacantly at nowhere."

The Africa to which Albert Schweitzer came is the same today — the same as the Africa of countless ages ago. Near the hospital, the river still teems with hippopotamuses, crocodiles, water snakes, fish of all kinds. Cranes and pelicans, ospreys and hawks, owls,

This baby white owl took shelter under the veranda roof. There was difficulty in feeding it, for it was afraid to come down for the fish spread out before it. But the Doctor finally succeeded in charming the fluffy little creature until it would eat from his hand the bits of meat which he had prepared for it.

parrots, and many other gaily feathered birds splash the air with color. The dark, impenetrable forest is alive with apes and leopards, panthers and buffaloes, boa constrictors and chimpanzees, gorillas and elephants.

The courtyard bordered by the houses of the white members of the staff is a miniature zoo. Since no animal is wantonly killed near the hospital (the natives finding it more profitable to bring them to Doctor Schweitzer, who always makes a "gift" in return), one never knows what animals will be found there. The domestic animals wander freely about: hens and chickens, geese, goats and African sheep, dogs and cats. But the wild animals are there, too. Always, under the doctor's house or in pens behind it, there are the antelopes. Monkeys scamper among the trees or on the corrugated roofs. The air is filled with the unmusical chatter of the weaver birds, busily stripping the fibre from the palm trees to make their spherical hanging nests — which they build close to the houses for protection from snakes. A white owl may be sitting under the piazza roof, or a pelican above the doctor's door, or a stork on the ridge pole. A porcupine may be lumbering around the yard, or a wild pig rooting about, its hungry eyes on the chickens. Among them all the doctor moves, with kindly, observing eye and generous hand, stopping to feed bits of meat to the white owl, or peel an orange for the antelopes, talk to the pelican, or smile at some chimpanzee's comical prank. At his heels are usually his dogs, splashed with the methylene blue that is used to combat the prevalent skin diseases.

This is the animal world of Albert Schweitzer.

There are no formal gardens at Lambarene: Doctor Schweitzer does not like gardens where flowers are grown for the adornment of the house. To cut a flower needlessly is a violation of his fundamental ethical principle of reverence for life. The flower, he believes, has the same right that we have to fulfill its natural life cycle. Respect its life, then — let it grow.

Once, when Doctor Schweitzer was walking with a friend in St. James Park in London, the other man suggested that they walk on the grass; the paths, having just been covered with fresh gravel, were a bit rough. But Doctor Schweitzer exclaimed: "What! Do you think that I would trample on the grass when there is any sort of a path to walk on!"[1]

Schweitzer's sense of comradeship extends to the humblest of creatures. I was sitting beside him just before dusk one day at Lambarene, two small antelopes, Léonie and Théodore, playing before him and two puppies, César and Hannibal, playing behind, when I noticed a black ant crawling up the white collar of his shirt. Without thinking, I reached up to brush it off.

"No, no!" said he, "that's my ant."

Once he dropped a spoonful of grapefruit juice on the floor and a swarm of little black ants crowded about thirstily to drink it up. "Look at my ants!" the doctor exclaimed with delight. "Just like cows around a pond!"[2]

Noel Gillespie, the young man who went out to help Schweitzer on his second trip to Africa, was putting on his raincoat one day when he saw a beetle, which had been eating holes in the coat and ruining it as a waterproof, fall to the ground. He started to step on it, when he felt a hand on his shoulder and heard Schweitzer say: "Gently, Noel! Remember you are a guest in its country."[3]

A guest in its country! In Africa, Schweitzer thinks of himself as a guest in a land which still belongs to the animals. Hard necessity sometimes compels him to take the lives of other creatures, but he never does so thoughtlessly, always with full, conscious acceptance of his painful responsibility.

One evening, just after my arrival at Lambarene, when the table had been cleared of the supper dishes, the quiet lamplight service had come to its peaceful end, and we were all feeling a sense of benediction there in the deep night of the African jungle, Doctor Schweitzer rose from the table to go to his room. On the way out, he stopped and took my arm.

"Come," said he, "I want you to meet my night watchman. He ought to know who you are."

I got my lantern and followed him across the compound to the steps leading to his veranda. We paused at the foot of the stairs.

---

[1] *Albert Schweitzer: The Man and His Mind,* by George Seaver (New York: Harper and Brothers, 1947), p. 291.

[2] Seaver, p. 291.

[3] *Albert Schweitzer: Life and Message,* by Magnus Ratter (Boston: The Beacon Press, 1950), p. 59.

"Here he is," said the doctor.

I looked around. There was no one in sight. I turned to the doctor in confusion. Even a dark-skinned Negro can be seen in the jungle night by the light of a lantern.

"Up there," said the doctor.

And there, above our heads, perched on a high trellis gate, was a huge pelican.

"Bon soir, Monsieur le Pélican!" said the doctor.

And the pelican flapped his great wings, thrust his long beak up in the air, and with several harsh, throaty expulsions of breath greeted his friend, the doctor.

"He is my night watchman," said Schweitzer. "Every evening at six o'clock, when the bells of the Catholic mission on the island out in the stream begin to toll, he flies up from his fishing down by the river, and takes his place on his perch for the night. And every morning, at six o'clock, when the bells awaken the mission, he spreads his great wings and is off again for his fish. But while he is there during the night, no one can pass up these steps except Mlle. Emma, who has a room in this house, and myself. Everyone else gets a powerful rap on the head. He is particularly hostile to the black women when they come up here into our courtyard. Apparently he thinks they have no place among the whites, and when they appear he chases them and attacks them with his beak. I have had to pay many a black woman two francs in atonement for his hostility. But he is a very faithful guardian, and very much of a personality."

He went on to tell the story of the pelican. A few years before, three young pelicans had been brought to him by some natives who had captured them somehow on the sandbanks and had taken them away from their parents. Their wings were not grown, and they were weak and hungry. So the doctor had taken them under his protection, made a house for them beneath the veranda, and tried to satisfy their voracious appetites until they were strong enough to care for themselves. At first the fish had to be put into their beaks, but later they learned to catch them when thrown. Little by little they grew and acquired feathers. One of them, smaller than the others and weaker, was slow in learning to fly, but at last he too was down on the river catching his own fish.

The dry season came, and down the stream from the inland waters came many other pelicans — for the great river was drying up, the sandbanks were emerging, and the fishing in front of the hospital was good. Soon the three pelicans that had been brought up at the hospital were circling with the others above the trees in great and beautiful winged flight. Then the rains came again and the waters rose swiftly among the palm trees on the shore. It was thought that all the pelicans would leave together for the smaller streams of the interior. But the pelican who had been backward in his development stayed behind when the others went. It was evident that he had learned to like the hospital, to feel a certain security there which he did not expect to find elsewhere. There was fish to be had from the kitchen as well as the river, and there was a fellowship with other life that he seemed to like. He became fond of the African sheep, which have fur instead of wool, and for hours at a time would stand perched on a stump among them, like St. Francis preaching to the animals. One of the big rams became a special friend and the two were often seen together.

So, season after season, the pelican has presided over the doctor's door at night, his self-appointed watchman. There is no doubt that some strange tie binds him to the doctor. With the dogs he has to be constantly on guard, and the black women, whose fish he steals, are his pet aversion. Yet he is content away from his fellow pelicans, with whom he mingles only when they return in the dry season to fish from the sandbanks. He has become a person of dignity around the hospital. He is Monsieur le Pélican.

Some months after I had left Lambarene, Schweitzer sent me the latest news about the pelican.

"Here," wrote the doctor, "is the pelican back again in his place above the veranda door. You heard that he had a broken leg and that he could not fly any more. For weeks we had to carry him from our house to the river and fetch him again in the evening, bringing him back to his place up here. Now he walks and flies again. It was certainly a native woman whom he was attacking to steal her fish who hurt him with a paddle while defending herself. Some day he will be killed that way. But meanwhile he is once more enjoying life."

Doctor Schweitzer hardly writes a letter to me without mention-

At night the pelican roosts at the top of the veranda steps that lead to the Doctor's room. There on his perch he guards the Doctor through the long hours of the tropical night. Woe betide any careless wanderer who comes within reach of his powerful beak. The Doctor he never molests.

He sits on the edge of the Doctor's stone pier and watches for the schools of little fish that come gliding down the river. Then he hops down into the shallow water beside the pier, where the fish cannot see him, and surprises them as they come into view, thrusting his long beak among them, lifting it into the air until the water has run out and then swallowing the fish he has caught.

Sometimes he rests above the pen where the antelopes are kept and surveys the busy life of the courtyard. The Doctor reaches up his hand to caress him.

During the day he is usually down in the river watching for fish in front of the hospital grounds.

ing some of his animal friends, who are, like his doctors and nurses, a part of the big hospital family, with their own personalities and their right to full consideration. In one letter to America he writes: "In my room at the moment there is a miniature antelope, Pamela. It is a special species which does not grow higher than thirty-five centimeters and is extremely graceful and intelligent." In a letter to Paris he writes: "In that clamorous, agitated Paris you will be homesick for the stillness of Lambarene. . . . This evening even the music of the crickets is *pianissimo* . . . Léonie, Théodore, Caro and the pelican send their greetings. Today there was a whole flock of pelicans on the sandbank."

Whenever Doctor Schweitzer returns to Europe, he is constantly mindful of the animal friends he has left behind him. On his upstairs work table at Gunsbach are two book ends — ebony elephants with ivory tusks. Directly in front of him, as he works, are two exquisite miniatures in watercolor, done by one of his nurses. Miss Gloria Coolidge, of Milton, Massachusetts. One of them shows Monsieur le Pélican perched on a stump rising from the river. The other shows two of his antelopes, Léonie and Lucie.

"As long as I am here I want those little framed pictures in front of me on my table," he said.

And there they are. Sometimes I have seen him take his place at the table and look at the pictures for a few moments, saying over and over again, "Léonie and Lucie! Léonie and Lucie! Léonie and Lucie!"

Behind him on the wall as he works at this table is a framed picture of a chimpanzee, on which Albert Schweitzer has written the words: "Julot, my Lambarene chimpanzee, now at Zürich Albert Schweitzer, 1936."

He never forgets these animals he has known and loved. At one time he had a Red River hog that used to wander around the hospital like a dog. Then, like all wild boars, she developed an appetite for the hospital hens. There were only these alternatives: she had either to be killed or sent to a zoo. It was decided to send her to a zoo. Later in London, Schweitzer went to see her. She was so sleek and glossy that Schweitzer hardly recognized her, but when he patted her, she gave him a grunt of recognition.

"Ah, Thekla," said he, "you have become a great lady of the

world, but I'm not so sure you wouldn't rather be eating our chickens still!"

Mrs. C. E. B. Russell tells of a wonderful evening spent at the organ with Doctor Schweitzer at his old church of St. Nicholas in Strassburg. It was in 1928. She was on her way back to Lambarene for her second visit there; he was setting off on a round of concerts and lectures in Western Europe. At her request he played Bach's *Prelude and Fugue in E minor* and, afterwards, the *Prelude and Fugue in C major*.

Then he switched off the light and said, "Now I'll play something for Canada." Canada was Mrs. Russell's pet monkey in Lambarene.

"So he proceeded," says Mrs. Russell, "to improvise more beautifully than I have ever heard him before or since. It was all full of the magic of the African forest, the moonlight in the jungle and on the river, the merry gambols of the monkeys in the trees when the sun is shining. . . . I think this organ recital, which lasted nearly two hours, was the loveliest of all I heard."[4]

C. F. Andrews, of India, met Schweitzer in England. The conversation was brief, for Schweitzer had to take a train from a London station. Andrews decided to accompany Schweitzer to the station, and they walked along, each carrying one end of a stick on which Schweitzer's German knapsack was slung. The train was already approaching the station. There was no time to lose, and they were hurrying along, when suddenly Schweitzer stopped, swinging Andrews almost off his feet, and exclaimed: "Ach, so!" He put down his end of the stick and tenderly picked up from a rut in the road a poor, half-frozen worm, which he carefully placed in the hedge-row. Then he came back, picked up his end of the stick again, explaining quite simply with a gentle smile that if it had remained there a few minutes longer it would certainly have been crushed by some auto traveling along the road. They hurried on to the station, where Schweitzer barely caught his train.

Another story tells how Doctor Schweitzer had gone in a big *pirogue* from the hospital to the steamboat landing in the town of Lambarene, which is on a great island in the river Ogowe. He had left the dugout half an hour's walk from the steamboat landing and had said good-bye to a doctor returning to Europe. Towards

---

[4] Ratter, pp. 112f.

This is the Doctor's cat, Sizi. Its mother disappeared when it was a kitten. The Doctor fed it by hand with a medicine dropper and saved its life. Every afternoon at 2:30, it comes to the Doctor's room to be fed. In the evening Sizi sits on the table in the pharmacy when the Doctor is writing prescriptions. Often it falls to sleep on the Doctor's left arm. The Doctor continues to write with his right hand, but he will not move his left arm while the cat is asleep on it.

midnight he returned to the place where the dugout had been left. Heavy rumblings of thunder in the black sky foretold the quick coming of one of those violent tornadoes which make the river dangerous for small boats. The dugout was shoved off, and the eight paddlers urged to hasten, that they might get home safely before the rains and the winds came. Then from the bank behind them they all heard the howling of a dog. Schweitzer insisted on going back again, in spite of everyone's protests and the imminent danger, to see what was wrong. As the dugout touched the bank again a dog sprang in, wagging his tail.

"He wants to come to the hospital," said Doctor Schweitzer, "so we must let him. Now paddle your fastest."

They arrived at the hospital just before the storm broke. Then, by the light of the lantern, they discovered that the dog had a bad case of scabies, and was covered with sores.

They gave the dog food and shelter, but all night long he yelped. In the morning a Negro orderly recognized the dog as belonging to someone living in the village on the other side of the river. The doctor gave instructions that the dog's open sores should be treated. He was tied under a palm tree and one of the nurses gave him exactly the same kind of treatment that was given at the hospital to human beings. He was carefully washed, a bright yellow sulphur ointment was applied where the skin was unbroken — over about half of the body — and the sores tenderly bathed with methylene blue, a soothing treatment which usually cures them in a day or two. The dog was very patient, and when it was all over, he jumped into the small *pirogue* which was to take him back to his village again, wagging his tail in visible gratitude. It is not recorded what his owner said or thought, when the dog, which had been all white, returned after a mysterious night's absence resplendent in purple and gold.

Dr. Schweitzer's relation with the animal world around him is a very vital one. He is full of concern for the well-being of all creatures, ready to sacrifice himself in every possible way that they may be helped. When one has seen him working late at night in the pharmacy, writing out prescriptions with his right hand, while his left arm goes to sleep because Sizi, his little cat, has cuddled up against it and must not be disturbed, one begins to understand the full measure of affection and sympathy which Schweitzer cherishes for the animals around him. It is not pure sentimentalism. It is something much more profound than that. He warned me once that I should not caress the hospital dogs, not even Tchu-tchu, his own special dog, who alone is allowed to enter the dining room and sit behind her master's chair. "There is dysentery at the hospital," he said. "The germs are in the dust. The dogs roll on the ground, and may have the germs in their fur. It is better not to touch them."

So, too, while he loves the wild animals, he does not forget that it is their nature to be wild. The antelope seems like a gentle creature, but no animal can be more dangerous at times. Once the doctor himself was seriously wounded by the horns of one of his antelopes. When his pets grow up, he has them put in a cage — a wise, realistic and unsentimental way of handling them.

In his philosophy, of course, Schweitzer had to find a place for animals. He found the answer he was groping for, appropriately enough, in the midst of a herd of hippopotamuses, while making a long canoe trip on an errand of mercy. Suddenly, there came to him, while he was wrestling in his mind with the problem of ethics, the phrase "reverence for life." This was for him the trail out of the jungle, the missing piece with which all his thinking fell into one lovely pattern.

"I am life that wills to live in the midst of other life that wills to live," he thought. "I must interpret the life about me as I interpret the life that is my own. My life is full of meaning to me. The life around me must be full of significance to itself. If I am to expect others to respect my life, then I must respect the other life I see, however strange it may be to mine. And not only other human life, but all kinds of life: life above mine, if there be such life; life below mine, as I know it to exist. Ethics in our western world has hitherto been largely limited to the relation of man to man. But that is a limited ethics. We need a boundless ethics which will include the animals also."

One day, years before, when he was sitting on the banks of the Rhine reading from a huge book of history, a little insect fluttered in between the pages and was almost crushed there. He spared the

There are usually a dozen dogs at the Lambarene Hospital. This one is the Doctor's own, Tchu-tchu. She has a very privileged position. She is the only dog permitted to follow the Doctor into the dining room. There she sits behind his chair and receives dainty morsels from his hand.

insect's life, saying to himself: "I am like that poor little midge, in danger of being crushed under the weight of history."[5]

In these later years Schweitzer has been striving to save mankind from being crushed under the weight of history, warning us in his *Philosophy of Civilization* of the doom towards which we march by abandoning all thinking and forfeiting our spiritual values. There is no civilization to take the place of this one, he cries, like a prophet in the wilderness; beware lest this one fall in ruins about us. So he has been striving, in similar fashion, to spare the little fluttering insect and all its animal kin by his teaching of reverence for life.

It is not an easy teaching. Schweitzer is no fool. He looks out into the universe and sees the deep night of unthinkable cruelty, as one species preys on another, and life feeds on life. Nothing daunted, however, he looks within the human heart and finds something of love there, something that shines out into the dark universe like a bright beacon, and in the shining of that light within he finds the evidence of God and the hope of a better future. He is well aware that he has not solved the riddle and that he himself is compelled at times to hurt and kill, but woe unto us if we needlessly hurt and kill.

In one of his letters from Lambarene in September, 1937, Schweitzer writes of the blue haze that envelopes the forest at that season of the year and the red glow around the horizon at night. The natives are burning the forest — the only way they have of getting rid of the huge trunks and making new plantations for their bananas and manioc. And then he adds: "When at this season of the year I see in the night skies the ruddy glow of the conflagrations, I am filled with pity for all the creatures of the forest consumed in the flames." Once we were walking together through some land which had been burned over on the other side of the river near the Catholic mission. He stopped and spoke of all the tragedies that had taken place in the devouring fire, and spoke of the old Chinese thinkers who considered it a crime to burn the forests because of the frightful death brought to so many living things. Yet Schweitzer is well aware that the natives are unable to cut up the huge trees which they fell, and which must be burned for the enriching ashes

---

[5] Ratter, p. 55.

left on the soil, taking the place of the manure which cattle and horses elsewhere provide. Otherwise, three years later, when the banana trees they could not plant would have borne, there is a famine in the land, and the people die of hunger. At the hospital every effort is made to cut up the great logs and drag them away from the land that is to be planted, but even there it has been necessary at times to burn the forest.

Such is the tragic necessity forced upon us. In Lambarene it has been hard to teach the natives that at the hospital not only human beings are healed and cared for, but the animals as well. It was with great difficulty that one of the nurses saved two porcupines from the bush knives of the hospital workmen. But on another occasion only two of them tried to kill an antelope that sprang up before them and ran for the woods: the others remembered the teaching of the old doctor.

Unfortunately, there are exceptions which confuse the simple native mind. Miss Hausknecht, one of the nurses, tells of one instance. As she was setting out young fruit trees, grasshoppers came along, devouring not only the foliage but even the fresh young shoots themselves. So she had been compelled to have a group of workmen pick off the grasshoppers and kill them. In amazement the workmen exclaimed: "But in the doctor's hospital no living thing is killed." Miss Hausknecht was overjoyed to find that the doctor's teaching had so gripped these savage hearts. Yet, for the sake of the breadfruit trees, she still had to exhort them to kill the grasshoppers.

Here in the doctor's own experience, right in his own hospital village, the fatal dilemma which we all face arises. There is no answer to this bleak problem. Doctor Schweitzer is not a vegetarian. There are times when he must take life. Indeed, his very task is to kill the worms that infest the bodies of the natives, to lay low the bacteria that cause so many diseases. Deliberately, consciously, he takes life — to save life; but always with wondering and questioning, always with a heavy heart.

To the principle of reverence for life he clings. It is the one precious thing that distinguishes the man from the brute. It must not be abandoned. Without it ethics is impossible. Here is the

Mademoiselle Koch, one of the faithful nurses, has a way with her parrots. They sit on the back of her chair, or on a perch beside her place at the table, waiting for her attention. The cats do not attack the parrots in the Doctor's village.

little gleaming fire of love which may some day, perhaps, warm the universe.

There is no danger of its being carried to an extreme. Keats once wrote a word about disinterestedness, which he said should be "carried to its highest pitch, as there is no fear of its ever injuring society — which it would do, I fear, pushed to an extremity. For in wild nature the hawk would lose its breakfast of robins, and the robin his of worms — the lion must starve as well as the swallow."

So Schweitzer, too, would say that disinterestedness, love, reverence for life must be carried to the highest possible pitch, if we are to emerge as ethical beings. And if sometimes we are forced to injure and destroy, let us do so with a full sense of our responsibility.

In the summer of 1949, when Schweitzer was traveling across the American prairies, he was told the story of the airlift that had carried food to the snowbound animals the preceding winter. "Ah," said he, "what a magnificent feat! *Vive l'Amérique!*"

Later, in Europe, Albert Schweitzer told me he believed there was more reverence for life in America than anywhere else in the world.

CHARLES R. JOY

Key to the Sources

Falkenjägerei — "Nochmals Falkenjägerei." Article in *Atlantis* (Zurich), March 1932.

Geschichten — *Afrikanische Geschichten.* Bern: Paul Haupt, 1939. Published in English as *African Notebook* (New York: Henry Holt and Company, 1939).

Gottesdienst — *Gottesdienst im Spital zu Lambarene.* Privately printed.

Indian — *Indian Thought and Its Development.* Translated by Mrs. Charles E. B. Russell. New York: Henry Holt and Company, 1936.

Jagd — *Afrikanische Jagdgeschichten.* Strasbourg: Editions des Sources, 1936.

Josephine — "Josephine das zahme Wildschwein." Article in *Schweizerisches Jahrbuch: Die Ernte.* Published by the Garbe-Schriftleitung. Basel: Friedrich Reinhardt, 1923.

Kindheit — *Aus meiner Kindheit und Jugendzeit.* Munich: C. H. Beck'sche Verlagsbuchhandlung, 1926. Published in English as *Memoirs of Childhood and Youth* (New York: The Macmillan Company, 1931).

Kultur — *Kultur und Ethik.* Munich: C. H. Beck'sche Verlagsbuchhandlung, 1923. Published in English as *Civilization and Ethics* (New York: The Macmillan Company, 1929), one volume of the work *Philosophy of Civilization.*

Leben — *Aus meinem Leben und Denken.* Leipzig: Felix Meiner Verlag, 1932. Published in English as *Out of My Life and Thought* (New York: Henry Holt and Company, 1933).

Lettres — *Lettres de l'Hôpital du Dr. Albert Schweitzer à Lambaréné.* Strasbourg: Imprimerie Alsacienne, 1930-1946.

Mitteilungen — *Mitteilungen aus Lambarene.* Series I, Bern: Paul Haupt, 1925. Series II, Strasbourg: Imprimerie

Alsacienne, 1926. Series III, Strasbourg: Imprimerie Alsacienne, 1928. Published in English as *The Forest Hospital at Lambarene* (New York: Henry Holt and Company, 1931). Later published in *On the Edge of the Primeval Forest* (New York: The Macmillan Company, 1949).

Protection   "Philosophy and the Movement for the Protection of Animals." Article in *The International Journal of Animal Protection* (Edinburgh), May 1935.

Regen   "Regen and schönes Wetter auf dem Aquator." Article in *Kirchenkalender*.

Reverence   "The Ethics of Reverence for Life." Article in *Christendom*, Vol. I, No. 2 (Winter 1936). From transcript of Dr. Schweitzer's Gifford Lectures made by Rev. Dwight C. Smith, edited and revised by Dr. Schweitzer.

Schlangen   "Im Lande der Schlangen." Article in *Evangelischer Familien Kalender für Elsass-Lothringen*, 1939.

Spital   *Das Spital im Urwald*. Bern: Paul Haupt, 1948.

Urwald   *Zwischen Wasser und Urwald*. Bern: Paul Haupt, 1926. Published in English as *On the Edge of the Primeval Forest* (New York: The Macmillan Company, 1931).

Weltanschauung   *Die Weltanschauung der indischen Denker*. Munich: C. H. Beck'sche Verlagsbuchhandlung, 1935. Published in English as *Indian Thought and Its Development* (New York: Henry Holt and Company, 1936).

Except for the three passages followed by the key words *Indian, Protection,* and *Reverence,* all the writings of Albert Schweitzer used in this volume have been newly translated by the editor.

Much of the material in this volume has never before appeared in English.

The following publishers have kindly given the editor permission to reprint existing translations or to make fresh ones: The Macmillan Company, Henry Holt and Company, Atlantis Verlag, *Christendom,* and *The International Journal of Animal Protection.*

PART I

IMPRESSIONS OF AN ALSATIAN CHILD

Impressions of an Alsatian Child

THE PASTOR'S BEEHIVE

From my earliest childhood I remember the first time I was conscious of shame for my own behavior. I was still wearing a little dress, and I was sitting on a small stool in the yard while my father busied himself with the beehive in the garden. A pretty little creature settled down on my hand and delightedly I watched it crawl about. But suddenly I began to scream. The little creature was a bee which had every reason to be angry at the pastor's taking the filled combs out of the beehive, and so had stung the pastor's little son in return.

At my outcry the whole family hurriedly assembled. Everyone pitied me. The maid took me in her arms and tried to comfort me with kisses. My mother reproached my father for not putting me into a safe place before he began to work at the beehive. I had become so interesting in my misfortune that I continued to cry with great satisfaction, until suddenly I noticed that I was still shedding tears without feeling any more pain. My conscience told me that I should now stop. But to remain interesting for a while longer I went on with my wailing and got more comforting, which I had ceased to need. I felt so badly about this, however, that I was miserable all day long.

How often, as a grown man, when I have been tempted to exaggerate the significance of what was happening to me, have I been warned by this experience.   [*Kindheit*, p. 3]

THE UNGRATEFUL CALF

One Sunday evening in the high tide of summer, as we were passing by the house of Jägle, the sacristan, he came up to my father, almost in tears, and recounted the story of his calf. He had raised a beautiful calf, which used to run after him like a dog. At the beginning of the summer he had taken it to the mountain pasture; and on that very Sunday he had been up to visit it. But the calf no longer recognized him. He was only a man like other men to it. This ingratitude had wounded him deeply. The calf should never come back to his shed, he said.

He sold it at once.   [*Kindheit*, p. 5]

THE MISERY OF ANIMALS

As long as I can remember, I have suffered because of the great misery I saw in the world. I never really knew the artless, youthful joy of living, and I believe that many children feel this way, even when outwardly they seem to be wholly happy and without a single care.

I used to suffer particularly because the poor animals must endure so much pain and want. The sight of an old, limping horse being dragged along by one man while another man struck him with a stick — he was being driven to the Colmar slaughterhouse —tortured me for weeks.   [*Kindheit*, p. 22]

A PRAYER FOR ALL LIVING CREATURES

It was wholly unreasonable to me — this was even before I had gone to school — that in my evening devotions I should pray only for men. So when my mother had prayed with me and kissed me goodnight, I used secretly to add another prayer which I had myself composed for all living creatures. It ran like this: "Dear God, guard and bless everything that breathes; keep it from all evil and give it quiet sleep.   [*Kindheit*, p. 23]

"THOU SHALT NOT KILL"

In my seventh or eighth year, I had an experience that made a deep impression upon me. Henry Bräsch and I had made slings out of strips of rubber with which we could hurl small stones. It was Passion Week in spring.

One Sunday morning he said to me: "Come on, let's go up the Rebberg to shoot birds."

This was a horrible proposal to me, but I dared not refuse for fear he would laugh at me. So we came to a tree which was still bare, and on which the birds were singing out gaily in the morning, without any fear of us. Then stooping over like an Indian on the hunt, my companion placed a pebble in the leather of his sling and stretched it. Obeying his peremptory glance I did the same, with frightful twinges of conscience, vowing firmly that I would shoot when he did. At that very moment the church bells began to sound, mingling with the song of the birds in the sunshine. It was the warning bell which came a half-hour before the main bell. For me it was a voice from heaven. I threw the sling down, scaring the birds away, so that they were safe from my companion's sling, and fled home. And ever afterwards when the bells of Passion Week ring out amidst the leafless trees in the sunshine I remember with moving gratitude how they rang into my heart at that time the commandment, "Thou shalt not kill."

From that day on I have had the courage to free myself from all fear of men. Whenever my deepest convictions were involved I paid less attention than before to the opinions of others. I tried to escape from the dread of being laughed at by my comrades.

The great experience of my childhood and youth was the influence of the commandment that we should not kill or torture. All other experiences pale before it.   [*Kindheit*, pp. 23-24]

LIKE AN ANIMAL TAMER

While I was still in the village school we had a yellow dog named Phylax. Like many other dogs he could not stand the sight of a uniform, and always went for the postman. As Phylax was given to biting and had already attacked a policeman, I was appointed to keep him in check at the time of the postman's arrival. I used to drive him into one corner of the yard with a switch and would not let him out until after the postman had gone again. What a proud feeling it gave me to stand like an animal tamer in front of the dog as he barked and bared his teeth, and to master him with blows, when he tried to break out of his corner!

But the feeling of pride did not last. When afterwards we sat down again as friends, I blamed myself for striking him. I knew that I could also have kept him away from the postman by taking hold of his collar and stroking him. But when the fateful hour returned once more I yielded to the intoxication of being an animal tamer.   [*Kindheit*, p. 24]

THE TROTTING HORSE

During the holidays our next-door neighbor let me drive his horse. His bay was rather old and narrow-chested; it was not good for him to trot much. But with a driver's passion I gave way again and again to the temptation of whipping him into a trot, even when I knew and felt that he was tired. Pride in driving a trotting horse infatuated me. And the man let me do it, "in order not to spoil my pleasure." But how my joy disappeared when we got home and I noticed, as the animal was being unharnessed, what I had not seen from the wagon, how his flanks were working! What good did it do for me to look into his weary eyes and silently beg for forgiveness? [*Kindheit,* pp. 24-25]

NEIGHBOR LÖSCHER'S DOG

Once when I was home for the Christmas holidays — I was at that time in the *gymnasium* — I was driving a sleigh. Out of neighbor Löscher's house came his dog, who was known to be vicious, and who sprang yelping at the horse. I thought I was justified in hitting him with a well-aimed snap of the whip, although it was evident that he was running after the sleigh only in play. My aim was too good. Hit in the eye, he rolled howling in the snow. His yelps of anguish echoed long in my ears. For weeks I could not rid myself of them. [*Kindheit,* p. 25]

TWICE I WENT FISHING

Twice, in the company of other boys, I went fishing with a rod. But then my horror at the mistreatment of the impaled worms — and at the tearing of the mouths of the fishes when they were caught — made it impossible for me to continue. Indeed, I even found the courage to dissuade others from fishing. [*Kindheit,* p. 25]

AN UNSHAKABLE CONVICTION

Out of such heart-breaking experiences that often shamed me there slowly arose in me the unshakable conviction that we had the right to bring pain and death to another being only in case of inescapable necessity, and that all of us must feel the horror that lies in thoughtless torturing and killing. This conviction has become increasingly dominant within me. I have become more and more certain that at bottom we all think so, and simply do not dare to admit it and practise it, because we are afraid that others will laugh at us for being sentimental, and because we have allowed our better feelings to be dulled.

I was sure that I would never again fear the reproach of sentimentality.   [*Kindheit,* pp. 25-26]

Part II

AFRICA AND ITS ANIMALS

1

The African Scene

NOW IT IS AFRICA!

River and primeval forest! Who could convey to others these impressions? We seem to be in a dream. Antediluvian landscapes that would elsewhere have seemed creations of fancy here become real. We cannot tell where the stream ends and the land begins. A mighty network of vine-clad roots pushes down into the river. Clumps of palm, in their midst deciduous trees with green boughs and majestic leaves, towering single trees, wide fields of papyrus rising with great, fan-like leaves higher than a man, dead and rotting trees reaching to heaven in the midst of the luxuriant greenery. . . . In every clearing, water mirrors glitter; at every turn, new tributaries of the river open out. A heron flies up heavily and settles down on a dead tree; little blue birds hover over the water; high up a pair of ospreys circle. There, hanging down from the palm branch and swinging, two monkey tails — there can be no mistake about it! The owners of the tails become visible. Surely now it is Africa!   [*Urwald,* pp. 21-22]

PEACE

Above the palm trees in front of my window a pale blue sky rises. A scarcely perceptible breeze comes up from the river. On the mown field our herd of goats browses, each of them accompanied by a white egret. Not a sound disturbs the peace.

[*Lettres,* No. 5, p. 1]

JUNGLE SOLITUDE

My table stands by the lattice door that leads to the veranda, so that I may get as much as possible of the light evening breeze. The palms rustle quietly while the crickets and toads make loud music. From the jungle come dreadful and sinister cries. Caramba, the faithful dog on the veranda, growls gently to let me know he is there. A tiny dwarf antelope lies at my feet under the table. In this solitude I try to give form to thoughts that have been stirring in me since 1900, and to help in the restoration of civilization. O solitude of the primeval forest, how can I ever thank you for what you have been to me!   [*Urwald,* pp. 142-43]

BLUE HAZE AND DEATH

For several days a blue haze has covered the forest, and at night a reddish glow appears on the horizon. Haze and glow come from the fires that are lighted each year during the dry season in order to clear new land for the plantations. After the twentieth of September, the rains begin. That is why they burn the fallen trees now. The conflagration lasts for weeks. Even when they are relatively dry, the mighty trunks are only slowly and partially consumed. The maize and bananas, therefore, usually grow in a veritable tangle of branches and half-charred trunks.

When at this season of the year I see in the evening sky the light of the conflagration I am filled with pity for all the forest fauna destroyed by the fire. In China the burning of forests used to be considered a crime, because so many living things were brought by it to a frightful death.

For the natives of the region, these fires have become a necessity, for they are not equipped with tools for cutting the timber and moreover would not know how to use all the wood that would be cut.   [*Lettres,* No. 11, p. 1]

WORSHIP IN THE OPEN AIR

I cannot expect my listeners to sit as still as the faithful in a European church. I do not mind if those who have their fireplaces between the two barracks cook their meals while they listen, if a mother washes and combs her child, if a man repairs the fish-net he has hung up under the roof of the barrack, if many another thing of the kind goes on. Even if a native takes advantage of the time to lay his head in a comrade's lap and have him go on a hunt through his

When the Doctor preaches to the natives at the Sunday services, an interpreter on each side, the animals are there also. The weaver birds chatter in the palms overhead, the monkeys scramble noisily on the iron roofs, the domestic animals — hens, geese, dogs, cats, turkeys, goats and sheep — wander in and out among the natives who have gathered to hear the strange gospel. The Doctor has paused for a moment, but the dog begins to speak to the animal world about him.

hair, I do not forbid it. There are always new people there. If I were always to rebuke them during the service of worship, the solemnity of the occasion would be much more disturbed than if I let them alone.

I take no notice even of the sheep and the goats that come and go in the midst of the congregation, bleating and locking horns, or of the many weaver birds that nest in the near-by trees and make such a noise that I must raise my voice. Not once do Mrs. Russell's two monkeys disturb me. They roam freely on Sundays and during the service jump about on the neighboring palm-trees or run around on the corrugated-iron roofs, only to settle down at last, when they are tired out, on the shoulder of their mistress.

Nevertheless, in spite of the commotion, this divine worship in the open air takes on a moving solemnity from the fact that the word of God reaches men who now hear it for the first time.

[Gottesdienst]

THE JUNGLE HOSPITAL

Lambarene lies a bit south of the equator, on the river Ogowe, two hundred and eighty kilometers from its mouth, in the colony of Gabun, which is a part of French Equatorial Africa.

It is imbedded in the jungle. As far as the eye can reach there are no fields or meadows; only forests and water-courses are to be seen. This is true of all the lower reaches of the Ogowe. On both sides and upstream the savannas enclose the jungle.

The place is small. The inhabitants number about twenty whites and four hundred natives. Beyond the number of its inhabitants it has some importance by virtue of its being the seat of a district governor, its post office and radio station, its eight trading posts managed by Europeans, and its position as one of the principal centers for the trade in okume wood, since 1909 the chief export of the Gabun.

My decision to locate a hospital at Lambarene dates from the year 1905. Through Alsatian missionaries who were working in the region of the Ogowe I learned how essential it was that medical help should be brought to the natives there. Following their advice I chose Lambarene as the place for the hospital because it was just about in the center of the district and was accessible by the water-ways from all directions.

In the spring of 1913 I realized my purpose. In April of that year my wife and I arrived in Lambarene with seven cases containing whatever was necessary to outfit the hospital. The site for the hospital and for a little dwelling house was placed at our disposal by the French Evangelical Missionary Society at their station in Andende, which lies on a branch of the Ogowe about four kilometers from Lambarene. The missionaries there received us with great friendliness and to the best of their ability assisted us in our enterprise.

In the course of the next few months there rose down by the river a hardwood barrack that provided space for a consultation room, an operating theater and a pharmacy. Around it big bamboo huts with leaf-tile roofs were erected to house native patients. There was room there for about forty sick persons and their attendants. For the patients here do not arrive at the hospital alone, you know, but bring with them members of their families or friends, who have paddled them here and will take them home again.

The white patients were accommodated as well as possible in our little house and in the houses of the missionaries.

Until November 1917, my wife and I worked in this hospital under many kinds of difficulties, like those which the First World War brought with it. I told about this first sojourn at Lambarene in my book, *On the Edge of the Primeval Forest*.

In February 1924, after I had recovered from a tedious illness and had accumulated by lectures and organ concerts in different lands sufficient means to pay off the hospital debts which had been incurred during the war and to resume the work once more, I returned to Lambarene. My wife could not accompany me, partly because of her health and partly because she had to devote herself to our little daughter. From 1929 on, however, she came back to Lambarene repeatedly for longer or shorter intervals. She spent the years of the Second World War here.

On my arrival in 1924, I found the building that sheltered the consultation room, the operating theater and the pharmacy still in rather good condition. But the large bamboo huts where the native patients were accommodated lay on the ground, and had to be rebuilt. As two Alsatian nurses, an Alsatian doctor and a Swiss doctor arrived within the next few months, I was able to devote myself to this rebuilding, and also to erect another small house with a corrugated-iron roof for the white patients.

But when the hospital had been rebuilt and was in full operation, I had to reconcile myself to the necessity of transferring it to a more spacious location away from the mission station. The land available at the station was enough to take care of only forty native patients and their attendants. During 1925, the forty became sixty, then eighty, then one hundred and even more, since the hospital was constantly becoming more widely known.

In the autumn of 1925, during a famine, a severe epidemic of amebic dysentery broke out; and the problem of accommodating the numerous patients in such a restricted space made itself fully felt. Sixty dysentery patients who were a dangerous source of infection for the other patients and for those who lived at the hospital should have been isolated — but this proved to be impossible. So that we might never find ourselves in such a predicament again and, in general, to have the space we needed, I had to decide to move the hospital about three kilometers upstream from the mission station, to a place where it could expand when necessary, and where we could plant a big enough garden, lay out a plantation, and keep the animals we needed — hens, ducks, goats and sheep.

After completing the formalities necessary for getting a grant of ninety hectares from the authorities, we began, towards the end of 1925, first to clear the forest and then to build.

For two years I now turned practically all the medical work over to the other doctors, so that I could act as builder, mason, and carpenter. I had a valuable helper in the skillful native carpenter Monenzalie. Twice, in the midst of the construction, experienced Swiss came to give me timely help. All the buildings of the new hospital were constructed of hardwood and covered with corrugated iron in such a way that twenty-five centimeters under the iron roof there was a wooden roof for protection against the heat.

On the twenty-first of January, 1927, enough buildings had been finished to permit the moving from the old hospital to the new. How happy the native patients were to be accommodated in airy rooms, furnished with beds made of boards instead of logs! We also knew how to prize the opportunity to live in more spacious rooms and to have enough space to store our supplies.

In the course of the year a succession of other buildings was added, one for native obstetrical patients, one for pulmonary diseases, one for white and another for black mental patients, a number of houses for the native personnel and sheds for the animals.

At the present moment there are forty-five buildings. They stand on land that slopes gently to the river and is covered with oil palms and mango trees.   [*Spital*, pp. 1 ff.]

RAIN AND FINE WEATHER ON THE EQUATOR

Rain and fine weather are no subjects for conversation here. Nobody keeps a thermometer to learn what the weather for the next day will be. No one needs to try his luck in weather predictions. For with us the weather is not something uncertain, and one day in a particular season is like every other. How does that happen?

Everyone knows what the tropics are. They mark the farthest latitude to which the sun moves to the north in the northern hemisphere during the summer, and to the south in the southern hemisphere during the winter. The region between these two terrestrial circles is called the tropics. North of the Tropic of Cancer the weather is determined by the meeting between the warm air coming from the tropics and the cold air blowing from the polar region of ice. The weather in the so-called temperate zone depends upon the unpredictable and changing cloud formations and the precipitation which arise from this meeting, and also from the meeting of the warm and cold ocean currents.

It is otherwise in the tropics. Here it is exclusively the movement of the sun back and forth between the Tropic of Cancer and the Tropic of Capricorn which determines the temperature and the rain or lack of it. In its journey to the north or to the south the sun draws after it, for reasons we cannot wholly explain, an enormous quantity of rain. This rain pours down upon the regions over which the sun stands in that season of the year. When the sun moves farther on, the rainy season stops and the dry season begins.

People who live some distance north or south of the equator have only two seasons, summer and winter, separated by two transitional seasons, spring and autumn; we, however, have summer twice and winter twice — or, rather, the rainy season twice and the dry season twice. When it is summer in the north and the sun stands far from the equator over the Tropic of Cancer and has drawn after it its mass of water, it is our dry season. At the time of the autumnal equinox the sun comes back to the equator and then passes over it to the south. The mass of water brought by the sun descends upon us in October and November in the form of heavy thunderstorms. At Christmas the sun is far to the south. Then once more it is the dry season for us. At the time of the vernal equinox the sun comes back again to the equator. Immediately the thunderstorms begin again and last until the sun has again passed north. After that the dry season comes again.

As Lambarene is not directly on the equator but about sixty kilometers south of it, the dry season which comes with the journey of the sun to the north is much longer than the one that follows its journey to the south. It lasts three or four months (June, July, August and September), while the other dry season lasts only one or two months (December and January).

It is interesting to note how sharply distinguished are the seasons to the north and south of the equator. If one of our missionaries, during the dry season, takes a journey of only a few day over the equator to the north, he finds himself in the northern rainy season; if he takes a similar journey during our rainy season, he comes after a few days into the northern dry season.

It is remarkable and yet unexplained that we never have continuous rains near the equator. The rainy season is like this: about three times a week between four o'clock in the afternoon and six in the morning there is a heavy downpour. We very seldom have morning rains, midday rains or whole days of rain. Last year I counted a total of six rainy days — and not one of these was an unbroken day of rain. Usually it rains only at night; during the day it is almost always beautiful, just as we liked it to be as children. When a storm comes one night, it is seldom followed by another on the following night. A storm does not usher in a series of rainy days but invariably stops after a few hours.

Things are very different farther north in the Camerouns. At times it rains there without a break for weeks on end.

Our weather conditions are therefore determined by the fact that Lambarene lies in the southern hemisphere but in the immediate vicinity of the equator.

In detail the year's cycle is as follows. At New Year's we find ourselves in the short dry season — which is also our summer. Christmas Day, when the sun is farthest to the south, is our St. John's Day. This little dry season is not entirely without rain: now and then a storm breaks. The heat is already great and increasing every day. February is our August. At the end of February, sometimes even earlier, our autumn rains begin. It does not grow colder, however, but warmer. At the time of the vernal equinox the sun stands directly over the equator. In these months complete calm is the rule. All day long not a single leaf on the trees stirs. Even at night it is frightfully hot, because the intense humidity on the earth's surface hinders its cooling.

As a result of the frequent storms the river rises and overflows the banks. But a flood causes no one any concern here. The waters cannot destroy fields and meadows, nor can they undermine streets and railway embankments — none of which exist here. All human settlements are situated on the heights.

At the end of March the swallows leave us; at the end of April the oranges, which blossomed in November, begin to ripen.

Toward the middle of May we look out on the morning mists which are supposed to herald the beginning of the dry season. They are usually sighted around the fifteenth of May. On the same day, at about eleven o'clock in the morning, one feels a light, cool breeze from the south, which may last perhaps only for a quarter of an hour. The days of terrific heat are now numbered. The tornadoes come more and more frequently. Moreover they bring more wind, lightning and thunder than rain. In the first half of June they cease entirely. Then the light, cool south wind begins to blow steadily.

Now one must set out the garden! Only in the dry season can we have a garden. In the stormy season plants are beaten into the ground by cloudbursts of rain and rot. And one must work fast! The garden must have borne its fruits before the October rains come again, or all the pains will have been taken in vain. How often has the cabbage rotted before we have had a single head of it in our kettles, because the rain began before it matured.

We cannot grow potatoes here: generally they flourish rankly without forming tubers. Nor does corn thrive. Vineyards are not to be thought of. Peas yield no crop.

We confine ourselves, therefore, to greens, beans, cabbages, radishes, carrots and tomatoes, although the latter seldom thrive. We often find, however, that the seeds ordered in Europe are ruined by the dampness, even when they are packed in well-sealed glass tubes. Then two or three weeks are lost and we have to procure seedlings from the other Europeans here.

As it does not rain, the garden must be watered daily. It is therefore usually laid out as close as possible to the river. And one has to be present himself when it is being watered, or the blacks to whom this task is turned over will be satisfied with moistening the ground superficially.

Banana groves and manioc shrubs defy the rain and bear the whole year through. It is not the fruit of the manioc shrub that is edible but rather the tuberous root.

Maize is set out at the beginning of both rainy seasons and ripens through them. We eat it as a green vegetable, in place of peas.

The oil palms and the breadfruit trees bear from October to June. During the dry season one rarely finds ripe fruit on them.

The old farmer's saying, "When the days begin to lengthen, the winter begins to come," holds true here, although our shortest day is St. John's Day. Then the sun is farthest away in the north. Of course, the difference between the short and the long days here amounts to only about twenty minutes. After St. John's Day, it begins to get cool, as we think of coolness. Now the shutters and doors in the barracks of the sick must be closed the whole night, as the people otherwise would begin to get cold toward morning, although the thermometer even in the night seldom falls below twenty degrees centigrade. Very seldom does it get cool enough during the day for me to think of putting on a khaki jacket. We usually go about here in shirtsleeves.

All plants do not behave alike in our summer and winter seasons. Many of them blossom at the beginning of the winter and bear their fruit at its end. The most important of these winter trees is the mango, with its big pear-shaped fruit; the only edible part is the fibrous pulp surrounding the huge stone in a thin layer and tasting something like turpentine.

At the end of June the sandbanks in the river begin to emerge. We are usually able to prepare our St. John's Day fire on some bit of a sandbank which has just appeared. As the swamps and the small watercourses now dry up, all the fish must return to the larger rivers. In July and August, therefore, the great catches of fish are taken in the shallow waters of these rivers with casting nets and dragnets. In general the fish caught are the middle-sized carp, which are immediately dried over great fires to preserve them.

In spite of the fact that now no rain falls for months at a time, the forest remains green. Even the grass does not entirely dry up. As the air is always humid, the ground does not give up its moisture. The shedding of leaves from the deciduous trees does not take place here all at once. Throughout the entire year the leaves fall and new ones take their place. The tree is never bare. On the mighty kapok trees one can see that some of the great branches are leafy and bear fruit while others are just beginning to leaf out and blossom.

We seldom see blue sky from the end of June until the end of July. It is usually gray, like an overcast November day at home. It is often so dark that one cannot read or write.

In August the sun begins to break through again. At the end of September very light evening rains set in. We are now constantly afraid that they may get heavier, for our garden still needs a fortnight to yield its produce. From the day when the first real storms come we eat up all the cabbage, even though only the tiniest of heads have formed — for otherwise it is now doomed to rot.

The fruits of the garden and the trees cannot be stored away. We think with envy of the farmers at home who, when autumn comes, bring their potatoes and their cabbages into the cellar and spread their apples and pears on straw.

Since one cannot store any provision of food here, the blacks have never gone in much for agriculture. The struggle for food has, of course, always made its claims upon them. On the other hand they have never felt great anxiety about it, as seems to be the lot of the Europeans. There are no failures in crops. Whoever plants his bananas, his manioc and his maize, and really takes the trouble to master the weeds in his plantation and to keep the wild boars and elephants away from it, can confidently expect a harvest. Potatoes and corn cannot be replaced. Therefore, the people here are not, as a matter of fact, properly nourished, particularly since they have no butter and no cheese. Milch cows cannot be kept here, on account of the tsetse fly. Even the goats thrive only when the European cares for them and diligently protects them from the mange which would otherwise destroy the herds.

By the beginning of September the cool breeze from the south pole has ceased. Hardly have the first heavier rains of October fallen when it again becomes unbearably hot. Each of us now begins to worry about how he will endure the eight hot months to come. Then the first swallows arrive from the north. They remind us of those who now have the greater anxiety of protecting themselves against the cold. How often I tell the blacks about the poor people in Europe who have to keep a fire going the whole day long and have to buy the necessary wood for it. They listen without comprehension. They cannot understand that there are no woods there where anyone can cut as much firewood as he pleases.

At Christmas, when the palm tree, instead of the Christmas fir, is decorated with lights, we are overcome with homesickness for the snow-covered woods and for the fields sleeping under their white blanket. Since nature never rests in the tropics, the people who live here never experience peace. If we get so much more exhausted here than in Europe, it is not simply because we suffer here under sun and heat, but also because we live in the midst of a never-resting nature.   [*Regen*]

2

Country of the Snakes

SNAKES OF ALL KINDS

We are richly blessed with snakes of all kinds on the Ogowe. If we have to use a narrow forest path it is a good plan to let two blacks go ahead with bushknives: from long practice they have a much better eye for snakes than we. This precaution is absolutely necessary when venturing into thick undergrowth.

To keep snakes as far as possible from the vicinity of a dwelling house, one must get rid of all bushes and keep the grass short, leaving no heaps of cut grass or chopped wood. Snakes do not like to stay where they find no shelter.

Different kinds of snakes are often found in trees, especially in palms. I have often seen snakes drop upon the corrugated-iron roof from the oil palms which shade my house. What particularly attracts the snakes to the trees is the bird nests. They travel from tree to tree by way of the branches. The birds therefore prefer trees that stand apart and offer more safety than the others. The weaver birds hang their nests on the extreme ends of the branches of isolated palms, which the snakes can climb only with great difficulty because of the thorns. Moreover, these birds nest preferably near human habitations, because they have learned that here there are fewer snakes.

Hens and ducks that run about freely near the house provide good protection, for they kill all kinds of young snakes and go after fairly large ones with courage. They rightly regard snakes as their worst enemies, for whom all kinds of birds and eggs are a coveted prey.

There is a snake here — not a very big one — that subsists principally on eggs. If it comes upon a brooding hen it eats the eggs out from under her. Extraordinary though it is, the hen does not flee but remains quietly sitting — with only a terrified cluck or two — on her eggs, as if she could protect them by continuing to cover them. After the snake has swallowed all the eggs it immediately goes to sleep on the ground, the devoured eggs in its body distinctly visible, like the beads of a rosary. So, very often, we succeed in killing it.

All the snakes like to glide into buildings, because they think they will have a good opportunity for rat-hunting there. I knew a white man who kept a dangerous and poisonous snake in his granary, and every day set out milk for it. He did not have a single rat in his house, and was sure that thieves would shun the place as well.

Because there is danger of snakes gliding stealthily into the house, people here customarily keep all the doors shut. We and the blacks who help in our house watch carefully to see that no door ever stays open even for a moment.

Some years ago at the Protestant mission station, a missionary one evening saw a snake come out from under a chest and disappear beneath the skirts of his wife, who was sitting on a chair in the middle of the room. Whispering to her to remain quite still, he got up cautiously, fetched a stick of wood and waited until he could see from the movement of the skirt folds on the floor — women still wore their skirts long — where the snake was. With a well-aimed blow, he hit it on the head, as his wife (who knew what it was all about without being told) sprang away that very moment to avoid being bitten by the injured reptile.

The principal poisonous snakes here are the so-called najas and vipers. We do not have cobras and rattlesnakes.

The najas can be recognized by the way in which, when aroused, they spread out the ribs of the neck, which are movable, in such a way that the skin between them looks like an oblong band — as though a narrow hood hung down under their heads. One of these snakes can spit its poison more than a meter, and thus it is called "spitting snake." On one's skin this poison does no harm, but if it gets in the eye, it produces an acute inflammation.

When traveling by boat, one must beware of a poisonous black snake with yellow stripes on its belly, which is very common here.

When going upstream it is the practice — in order to take advantage of the weakest current, and also to get some protection from the sun — to keep one's boat as close as possible to the shore under the overhanging branches of the trees and bushes. It happens time and again that this poisonous black-and-yellow snake, which can grow as long as three meters, will throw itself, from some branch where it is lying in wait for birds, into a boat passing underneath. In terror the passengers will throw themselves into the water, and many a native who could not swim has drowned in this way; or the boat may be capsized by the movements of the frightened people.

South America also has poisonous snakes which similarly endanger passengers on boats. In general there is a close relationship between the snakes of tropical America and the snakes of tropical Africa.

No white or black man has yet explained to me why the snake throws itself from the boughs into the canoe. It is not likely that it intends to attack the passengers. Most of the snakes here have an inexplicable inclination to let themselves fall down from trees. Recently one fell in the midst of some blacks who were breaking stones under the palms near my house.

The poisonous black snake with the yellow stripes on its belly is very often found near dwellings. I once discovered one in our courtyard under a pile of boards which had been lying there for some time during the construction of a building.

If one comes near them, the snakes of the naja variety will rear their heads and prepare to defend themselves, and it is thus that one often first becomes aware of their presence.

Among the poisonous snakes belonging to the viper family there is a rather small one of a green color which is found especially on clumps of bananas. Since it is not big and is hardly to be distinguished from the green of the banana leaf, one often discovers it for the first time when one is on the point of putting a hand on it.

Most of all we fear the horned viper, a short, monstrous snake not more than a meter and a half long, its body ending in a short stump of tail. It gets its name from two hard, scaly excrescences which stand out like horns on the front of its flat, three-cornered head. It usually lives near water and is a good swimmer. We are afraid of it not only because its bite is dangerous, but also because

it is so inconspicuous. One may discover other snakes when they take to flight or rear up to defend themselves, but the horned viper remains so still at the approach of a person that one may sometimes step over it without its moving. But if one alarms or disturbs it, it will strike with a terrifying rapidity that allows no escape.

Once after sundown I saw two horned vipers lying on a much-trodden path along the river in Lambarene. They were warming themselves in the still-hot sand. Had not a black called my attention to them, I should have taken them for two broken boughs and approached them unsuspectingly.

The horned viper usually lurks under fallen leaves, only its brown head protruding. It is not disturbed by approaching footsteps. The white man would step on it, if he were not warned by the black man going before him. The latter with his sharp eyes sees the head of the dangerous creature and at the last moment jumps over it with a leap.

Once a black has caught sight of a horned viper, it is usually done for. It is not agile and cannot easily defend itself against its attackers, who cut it to pieces with their bushknives; but it will sometimes make the first lunge.

The python or boa constrictor is one of the foremost among the non-poisonous snakes. The boa constrictor can be as much as eight meters long, and as much as seventy centimeters in circumference; but these large specimens are a rarity. Like the horned viper the boa constrictor is an excellent swimmer.

Its speed is one of its chief characteristics. I once saw a young boa constrictor about three meters long pursue a hen, with a fairly well-grown brood of chicks, along a path at the Protestant mission station. Although they ran as fast as they could, the snake was still faster and would very shortly have overtaken them if I had not hurried up with a long pole and driven it away. Before I could get to it, it had vanished in the deep grass.

When the boa constrictor reaches its full length, it may even attack a man, darting up with a hissing sound.

Once I sent some people to cut wood in the forest behind the hospital, under the direction of my hospital orderly, Dominik. After a short time they were back without the wood but dragging a five-meter boa constrictor with a liana. It had suddenly shot up among them as they were beginning to cut wood. They fell upon it with bushknives and axes, but in spite of its wounds the creature would not give in — laying about it in the air with its upreared body. It was a well-directed blow in the neck from Dominik's bush-knife that at last brought it low.

A boa constrictor once killed one of my finest goats. The goat-herd, with other blacks, followed its trail and managed to surprise and kill it. It was only five meters long, but it had swallowed the goat. The blacks then proceeded to eat both snake and goat.

Hen houses have a great attraction for boa constrictors, as well as for leopards. A boa constrictor one night got into a hen house at a mission station through a hole in the leaf roof, and slaughtered the hens in a frightful fashion. Having eaten so ravenously, it was too swollen to get out again by way of the hole it had used to get in. In the morning the children of the mission school found it under some boards which happened to lie in the hen house. They shut the door and ran to get something to kill it with. But before they could come back, the snake had vomited up the hens in its body and slipped out through the hole in the roof. The courageous children hunted it down and killed it, although they were dealing with a huge creature.

Customarily the boa constrictor pays with its life for breaking into a hen house. Since it can no longer get out of the hole through which it came, because of the hens it has eaten, it is a condemned prisoner. It often falls asleep after a meal and so is killed while sleeping.

Goats and sheep shut up in a pen are in constant danger of falling victim to the boa constrictor, particularly in places near the water.

A European I knew had a herd of goats on a little island on one of the many lakes in the Ogowe region. Time and again he would lose animals to a boa constrictor without ever catching sight of it so that he could shoot it. One morning his blacks told him that the snake had crushed one of the goats to death near a creek, dragged it into the bushes and left it lying there. (Often a boa constrictor will not immediately swallow its prey, perhaps because it is not yet very hungry or because it will be better able to swallow the carcass after it has decomposed and become more tender.

Even for a boa constrictor, swallowing a big animal is an effort.)

The white man left the poor goat, already completely crushed, lying there; but in its neck, with a strong fishhook, he fastened a wire rope, securing the other end to a palm tree. In the night the snake came and swallowed the goat, beginning as usual with the head. The horns gave the reptile no trouble, for the boa constrictor has digestive fluids which soften even horn when it is immersed in them for a certain time. But the fishhook it could not digest. In the morning the white man found the snake lashing around in the grass, trying vainly to free itself from the wire rope. A shot in the head put an end to its torment. It was something more than six meters long.

If one does not have a fishhook, it is enough to wind a wire rope around the neck of the animal which the boa constrictor has crushed and left to eat later. Before entirely digesting its prey it cannot free itself from the swallowed wire rope.

It does no good to set out some dead animal in order to catch the boa constrictor: it will swallow only what it has itself crushed and killed.

From a white I had befriended, I learned how a boa constrictor had attacked a native child. A black woman was returning to the village from the plantation along a narrow path, a dog and the child walking ahead. A boa constrictor lurking in the bushes, probably on the lookout for antelopes, allowed the dog to pass in order to throw itself upon the child, winding itself around him in a trice to crush him. The brave mother threw down the load she was carrying, seized a big bushknife and struck at the snake, so that it let the child go and disappeared into the bushes, bleeding from several wounds. But the mother's blows had severely wounded the child himself. Placing the child on her shoulder, she ran to a white man living near-by, arriving just in time for him to save the child from bleeding to death. It was this white man who told me of the incident.

This same white man one day happened to shoot at a magnificent snake lying on the branch of a tree and was amazed to see it still lying there quietly despite its wound. He went nearer and found that it was an empty skin a snake had cast off and left behind.

A few years ago, in the dry season, the natives set fire to a grassy meadow near the hospital, and the fire thereupon spread to an adjoining dry papyrus swamp. Afterwards they found in the swamp the charred head of a mighty boa constrictor.

In the water, also, there are snakes of which one must beware. I know of two natives who, in a little dugout in the inlet of a lake, were pursued by two angry snakes. The snakes, overtaking the dugout, threw themselves into it, even though the natives struck at them with their paddles. Help arrived just in time from shore, where the battle had been noticed.

Some time ago I heard cries from natives on the bank of the river twenty meters away from my house. When I hurried down I found men striking the water with long paddles, which they had at hand, while others were throwing stones. Not in the least bothered by this activity, a snake of about two meters tried again and again to get to the spot where it had attacked two washerwomen. Probably it lived under the stones which lay in the water at that point, and had been angered at being disturbed by the washerwomen.

The water snakes prefer to hang around banks frequented by human beings. There they find many opportunities for preying on fish attracted to such spots by the oil-soaked fibers of the palm nuts left over in the preparation of palm oil, and by refuse always being thrown into the water. Even on the river banks by my hospital snakes are constantly to be found. Newly arrived doctors and nurses have to be reminded to be careful near the shore, particularly after dark. But only after they have actually come upon snakes there do they take the warning seriously.

Once as one of the hospital nurses was stepping into our motorboat she was pulled back by the blacks who were to accompany her on the journey. They had discovered a snake under the bank close to the motorboat. Aroused from its rest, it jumped into the water with one rapid leap.

Many a fine dog falls a victim to snakes. Exercising their duty as guardians, they attack the snakes without being aware of the danger that threatens them. They are not well equipped for battle with this enemy. Hens with their beaks and their coats of protective feathers are better equipped in this respect than dogs.

During the last year two dogs which had grown up on my place and then been given away have been killed by snakes. One of them was defending its master's house against a poisonous snake that was trying to get in; the other was crushed by a half-grown boa constrictor which it had surprised by accident in the reeds.

There would be a good many more snakes here if they did not eat each other up. In this, the non-poisonous snakes do not have to fear the poisonous, since the former, like the hedgehog, are almost immune to the poison of the latter.

Considering the many poisonous snakes to be found here, the number of human beings bitten by them is not considerable, so far as my knowledge goes. This is to be explained by the fact that for the blacks the caution imposed upon them from childhood is almost automatic; and the whites, as soon as they have come upon snakes several times, or have had an opportunity to contemplate the lopped-off head of a horned viper, learn to imitate the blacks. Still I have, in a number of cases over the years, had occasion to employ serum for poisonous snake bite, thereby saving men from death.

[*Schlangen*]

SNAKE BITES

We often have cases of snake bite. Since it is hard to know whether the snake was poisonous or not, we give everyone an injection of anti-venom serum from the Pasteur Institute. One native, who came to the hospital too late after he had been bitten, had to have his gangrenous arm amputated.   [*Lettres*, No. 11, p. 4]

DAINTY MORSELS

Near the girls' school, Mr. Morel killed a boa constrictor. As it was shot with my gun I properly received half of it for the hospital. Unfortunately it was only five and a half meters long. When the dainty morsels were divided there was almost a fight among the patients.   [*Mitteilungen*, I, p. 41]

3

Tales of African Hunting

HUNTING TALES

I am not a hunter myself. But I have been regaled at my table with so many stories of hunting from the lumber exploiters who were being treated by me that I can tell hunting tales. I can tell them accurately, also, for many of them I have heard a half dozen times.   [*Jagd*, p. 1]

A HUNTING PARADOX

What of the shooting? In the real jungle hunting is futile. There is wild game, of course. But how is the hunter to see it and pursue it in the thick undergrowth? Good hunting is only to be found where treeless marshes and grassland alternate with the forest. But in such places there is usually no timber to cut. So here is the paradox: nowhere can one starve so easily as in the luxuriant vegetation of the game-filled forests of equatorial Africa!

[*Urwald*, p. 95]

TRADER HORN

When Trader Horn begins to tell about his adventures with wild animals, he seems at times to give free rein to his imagination. He is likewise rather irresponsible now and then in describing the habits of the wild animals. For example, he has the crocodile digging passages through the bank out of the water. But only the real cayman does that.

Leopards, elephants, hippopotamuses, buffaloes, crocodiles, boa constrictors, chimpanzees and gorillas are just as plentiful today as in his time.   [*Geschichten*, pp. 4-5]

74

Protecting the Animals

The newspapers inform us that there is now meeting at London a "Conference for the Protection of Wild Animals in Africa," in which all those powers that have African possessions are participating. The wild animals of our region do not need to concern these men very long; they are protecting themselves very well without help. In the depths of the jungles and marshes they are growing and multiplying to the point of becoming, in many districts, a veritable scourge for the population. The workers in many a logging camp go about their business in constant fear of elephants and gorillas.   [*Lettres,* No. 5, p. 6]

Dying in the Presence of Food

A man in the famine region, I was told, had a black hunter who used to kill much game with his rifle. When the famine broke out, instead of going out to hunt with increased zeal, he squatted with the others in the hut, to die of hunger with them, when he could have saved them with the ammunition his master had given him. Bananas and manioc are necessary for food, one cannot live without them — hypnotized by this logic, hundreds upon hundreds are now resigning themselves to death in this district.

[*Mitteilungen,* II, p. 54]

The African Buffalo

An American hunter had an extraordinary experience with a buffalo. He had fired at it and missed it. As he had no more bullets in his gun there was nothing left to do but run for it. Quickly, however, he was overtaken by the buffalo. For a full quarter of an hour they raced around a tree, one after the other. When the American could not take another step he decided to seize the buffalo by the horns and throw it, as the American cowboys do. He dared to do this because he had the strength of a Hercules and had once been a cowboy. But the African buffalo cannot be thrown in this American fashion. So they both danced around together, until, just as his strength came to an end, the Negroes employed by the American came running up and freed him from the buffalo.

This same American, in the company of another white, once got lost while hunting. For three days they waded through one swamp after another, without finding anything whatever to eat. The nights were spent in a downpour of rain. When they were almost too exhausted to proceed, a Negro in their company succeeded in getting his bearings from the shape of a tree which he saw in the distance. It turned out that they had been wandering about not far from their own clearings in the forest.

When he was brought to me sick, the Herculean American was a wretched skeleton. I had no difficulty in lifting him out of the boat and carrying him to the stretcher.   [*Jagd,* pp. 7-8]

WISDOM IN FLIGHT

All the distinguished hunters I know are very cautious and are not ashamed to tell how at one time or another they thought it the better part of wisdom to seek safety from danger in flight. All of them impress upon newcomers the need of taking the greatest care. How many have received excellent instruction in this matter at my table!   [*Jagd,* p. 8]

THE WHITE HERON

Unfortunately there are still hunters who pursue the white heron, whose feathers are much sought after in Europe for hat ornaments. More and more these poor birds are withdrawing into the remote and inaccessible stretches of water where they might hope to remain unmolested. They are hardly ever seen now on the river.   [*Jagd,* p. 9]

A POOR SPORTSMAN

At the home of Mr. Cadier, the missionary, we ate the flesh of monkeys for the first time. Mr. Cadier is a great hunter.

The blacks are rather displeased with me, because I use my rifle so little. When on one journey we passed an alligator asleep on the stump of a tree rising out of the water and I just watched it instead of shooting it, that was the limit for them.

"Nothing at all ever happens with you," the paddlers complained through their spokesman. "If we had been with Mr. Cadier, he would have shot for us long ago one or two monkeys and some birds

to provide us with meat. But you go right by an alligator and leave your rifle lying there quietly beside you!"

Their reproach rested lightly on me. I never want to shoot the birds that circle above the water. Monkeys are wholly safe from my rifle. One can often kill or wound three or four of them, one after the other, without ever getting them. They remain hanging in the thick tree branches, or fall into the bushes of the impenetrable swamp. And if one does reach them, one often finds a poor little baby monkey clinging with pitiful cries to its mother's body, already growing cold.

My main reason for keeping a rifle is to shoot the snakes, of which we have a great many in the grass around my house, and to kill the birds of prey that plunder the nests of the weaver birds in the palms in front of it.   [*Urwald,* pp. 68-69]

MONKEY MEAT

Since the war began we have become accustomed to monkey meat. One of the missionaries at the station, who employs a black hunter, regularly sends us some of his game. The hunter usually shoots only monkeys, since they are the game that can be most easily brought down.

Monkey flesh tastes something like goat flesh, only sweeter. One may think what he pleases about Darwinism and the descent of man; the prejudice against the meat of monkeys is not so easy to get rid of.

"Doctor," said a white man to me recently, "eating the meat of monkeys is the first step towards cannibalism."   [*Urwald,* p. 145]

4

The Elephant

The problem of getting food for the sick troubles me. There is almost a famine here — because of the elephants. In Europe people suppose that wild animals begin to die out when "civilization" arrives. This may happen in some regions, but in others almost the opposite may occur. Why? For three reasons. When the native population diminishes, as is the case in many places, there is less hunting. Moreover, the hunting is less successful. The natives have forgotten how to trap the animals in the primitive but still often very ingenious ways of their forefathers. They have become accustomed to hunt with the gun. In view of the possibility of eventual uprisings, however, the natives have, for years, been given very little powder by any of the states in equatorial Africa. In addition they are not allowed to possess modern hunting guns, but only old flintlocks. Thirdly, the war on wild animals is less energetically carried on, as the natives no longer have time for it. They can earn more money by felling timber and rafting than by hunting. So the elephants can thrive and increase almost unmolested.

We are now beginning to feel this here. The banana plantations in the villages northwest of us, from which we get our provisions, are continually frequented by elephants. Twenty head suffice to lay waste a great plantation in one night. What they do not eat they trample down.

The elephants are a danger not simply to the plantations, but also to the telegraph line. The line that runs from N'Djole into the interior bears testimony to this. The long, straight forest clearings that mark its course are in themselves very enticing to the animals. The straight, smooth posts, however, which seem expressly made for pachyderms to rub against, are irresistible. But the posts do not all stand very firm. If the pressure against them is too great, they fall to the ground. And there are always others in the same vicinity. So a strong elephant in a single night can bring down a whole stretch of telegraph line, and days may go by before the crew from the nearest station has found the damage and repaired it.

Although the elephants roaming the vicinity cause me much anxiety so far as the feeding of the patients is concerned, I have not yet seen one, and probably never shall. During the day they stay in unapproachable swamps waiting to plunder, at night, the plantations which they have previously reconnoitred.

A native who is here because of his wife's heart and is good at wood carving cut out an elephant for me. While I was admiring the primitive artistry I ventured to remark that the body perhaps had not been accurately designed. The insulted artist shrugged his shoulders.

"Do you think you can teach me what an elephant looks like? I once lay under an elephant that was trying to trample me to death."

The artist was indeed a famous elephant hunter. The natives slip up to within ten paces of the elephant, when they are hunting him, and then discharge their flintlocks at him. If the shot is not fatal and they are discovered by the animal they find themselves in a very unfortunate position. [*Urwald,* pp. 133ff.]

THE ELEPHANT'S ACHILLES HEEL

An encounter with an elephant ended disastrously for one of the natives. In the neighborhood of Samkita the elephant came to a place where mahogany was being felled. At the sight of the men he made a leisurely retreat. Then the woodcutters decided to kill the animal in the manner of their forefathers, by slipping up behind him and cutting with their bushknives the Achilles tendons of his hind legs. How many thousands of elephants in the forests of Central Africa had been rendered helpless in this cunning way and then tortured to death! But the blacks of Samkita lacked the skill which their forefathers had. The elephant became aware of the plot and charged them. The nearest of them he tossed into the air and, having bored through the body with his tusks, quietly jogged off. The injuries were so serious that we could not save the poor man's life.   [*Mitteilungen*, III, p. 29]

POTENT CHARMS

To acquire magic power the native goes to a great fetishman, who imparts to him the desired knowledge and makes him pass through successive rites of initiation.

No potent charm can be made without the sacrifice of a human life. How many men were slain in earlier days in this country because hunters wanted to fashion mighty charms for their elephant hunting! In the powerful fetishes, which I happened to see because they were handed over to the missionaries by Christians, there was always to be found a bit of the human skull.

[*Geschichten*, pp. 56-57]

THE HUMAN SKULL

The professional black elephant hunters are rather mysterious people. For the belief exists among the Negroes that a powerful fetish is required for every elephant killing. The most powerful fetish of all, however, is to be found in the skull of a man killed expressly for this purpose. There is, therefore, the danger that the black elephant hunter will commit murder to obtain the necessary fetish. A white man told me he had never accepted the services offered him by an excellent black elephant hunter, because he suspected that he would not shrink from murder to get a good fetish.   [*Jagd*, p. 4]

ELEPHANT STORIES

The elephant is not hunted in our country for the sake of the ivory. Although this has a very high value, it would still not compensate for the hardships of elephant hunting. The elephant is hunted for the sake of the meat, and because he destroys the banana plantations. The meat is smoked on the spot, and then carried to the villages where it is sold for a good price. Sometimes, however, when the news of an elephant killing spreads, so many people who fancy elephant meat hurry to the place that the meat does not even get smoked. Once when an elephant was killed in the vicinity of a white lumber exploiter's place, the hundred and

fifty black workers employed there swarmed over the animal and completely consumed it in two and a half days. One of them got a bone stuck in his throat and because of the danger of choking had to be brought to me in a hurry. It was in this way that I learned of the feast. [*Jagd*, pp. 3-4]

Taming the Elephant

It is usually said that the African elephant cannot be tamed and in this respect differs greatly from the Indian elephant. This is not completely true. I recall a tame elephant in the neighborhood of Cape Lopez, who pulled a cart and did other chores on a plantation. He was indeed so civilized that when the noon bell sounded he could not be moved to do another stroke of work. If he happened to be carrying a beam in his trunk he would, at the first clang of the bell, throw it to the ground.

On a plantation above Samkita there is an eight-year-old elephant named Sophie. She is very familiar with everyone. With a qualified trainer she would certainly have been taught to work. But here there are no such people as there are in India to train elephants. Therefore this elephant has become a veritable good-for-nothing. She is the terror of the gardener, whose greens and beans she pulls up. At times she amuses herself by uprooting dozens of cocoa trees. Another trick of hers is to open the hen house.

A few months ago it was planned to sell her to a zoo in Europe. A buyer was found immediately. Sophie was invited to take a walk to the river, where a steamer lay with a powerful crane. She was much pleased with the walk. As she was about to go over the straps of the crane, however, she became suspicious. So a couple of dozen Negroes were summoned to shove and pull her. The affair might indeed have drawn to a successful conclusion, given Sophie's generous good nature, if the engine had not, at the critical moment, let off steam. At this strange noise the elephant rose bolt upright and the Negroes who had been hanging on to her ran away and threw themselves into the water. One of them stumbled over a root and got a bad, earth-contaminated fracture, so that he had to be brought to my hospital immediately. He has been in our care since, and we hope to save his leg.

Sophie, however, went quietly home, and appears again in the plantation inventory under this entry: "Sophie, female elephant; eight years old; value, twenty thousand francs; destructive animal; monthly damages, one hundred and fifty francs."

[*Jagd*, pp. 4-5]

5

The Hippopotamus

Hunting the Hippopotamus

The hippopotamus is hunted for the sake of the meat. The genuine hunter never shoots at a hippopotamus for fun. It makes no sense to send bullets, as new arrivals do, into a herd of hippopotamuses from a river steamer. For the animals become very dangerous when they are merely wounded and will then attack small boats in blind fury, capsize them to get at the swimmers, grinding up their victims' arms and legs with their powerful teeth. The animals that are killed, on the other hand, sink in the water and are lost.

The real hunter shoots the hippopotamus only when he has time and opportunity to get the meat. For when the dead hippopotamus sinks, twelve hours elapse before it comes to the surface again as a result of the swelling caused by the gases of decomposition. Therefore, if the hippopotamus is killed in the river, the boat must remain in the vicinity of the place where the animal went down for twelve hours, and sometimes much longer, in order to sight the body the moment it rises and so salvage it. If in the meanwhile night has fallen, the prey may float away unnoticed and so be lost to the hunter. Sooner or later, however, people down the stream will discover it and have a happy time over it. For even if the meat is already green and stinking a festival will take place.

Our Negroes do not loathe bad meat. It is eaten with relish and, strangely enough, with impunity. A lady who recently arrived asked a Negro how he could eat such stinking meat.

He replied, "You know, it is the meat we eat, and not the smell."

It is best, then, to kill the hippopotamus when it is on the land. This is very perilous, however. The wounded animal immediately charges the hunter, and in spite of its ponderous body is more than a match for him in speed. A hippopotamus is seldom killed with the first bullet. A hunter must have great faith in his skill to waylay a hippopotamus on land.

The hippopotamus is in the water all day long. When darkness falls it comes out on the land and always in exactly the same spot. The bank is often worn away by the stomachs of the animals as they work their way up on the shore. So it is not difficult to find the hippopotamus; it is the waiting that takes courage.

The people of a village once told two whites, who had not been here very long and were not distinguished hunters, about the hippopotamuses who were in the habit of coming out on the land somewhere above their village; in the hope of having a fine feast they asked the whites to kill them. At sunset the whites went to the place. It grew dark. They could hear the snorting of the approaching hippopotamuses in the river. The hunters asked the Negroes who were lying in wait with them some questions but received no answer — they had quietly slipped away. Then they heard the two hippopotamuses working their way up the bank.

"Are you still there?" whispered one hunter to the other.

"Yes," the answer came, "but not for long."

And when the first man began to grope for the second, the latter's place was already empty. So the first man followed the example of the second as quickly as possible, while the bushes cracked under the feet of the hippopotamuses.

Two other hunters, also newcomers, made what they thought was a very wise plan. They discovered in a clearing the track of hippopotamuses climbing up on the land; they also saw two young trees which could be easily climbed, and in which they planned to wait for the animals in the moonlight. As soon as they heard the animals in the distance they bravely climbed up the trees and awaited whatever might come. After a few minutes one of them began to stir in his tree and groan.

"Keep quiet there," whispered the other man.

"I can't."

"Why can't you?"

"Ants."

He had chanced upon a tree inhabited by the notorious black ants.

"Here come the hippopotamuses!" said the other. "Hold out for a moment."

But the ants were the stronger. The white man threw his gun down from the tree, and sprang after it. The hippopotamuses, alarmed by the noise, threw themselves in the water.

For a whole year a malicious hippopotamus made a branch of the river leading to a certain lake perilous, by attacking every boat. Ten men had already fallen victim to it, and no one had succeeded in killing it. One day an American was traveling along that branch of the river to get food for the people in the forest where he was cutting timber. Like a good marksman, he had placed his Mauser between his knees ready to fire, but then he had fallen asleep. Suddenly the Negroes with him roused him. Five meters in front of the boat the dreaded hippopotamus emerged in order to upset the boat with a single blow of its body. But instantly it got a bullet in its head.

This feat brought the marksman great fame in the whole region round about. I almost came into possession of the teeth of this hippopotamus myself. The American intended to give them to me as a mark of appreciation for the care I had given him during a serious illness. But when he left Africa in his search for health he forgot, and I did not dare remind him of it.   [*Jagd*, pp. 5-7]

HIPPOPOTAMUS! BEWARE!

One misty morning, two hours before dawn, we started off. In the bow the two missionaries and I sat one behind another on long folding chairs. Amidships were heaped the tin trunks, folding cots, mattresses, and provisions for the Negroes' journey — bananas. In the stern in two rows of six each stood the twelve paddlers, one behind another. They sang about the end of the journey and about the people on board. Complaints about having had to begin work so early and having so hard a day before them were interwoven with their song.

The sixty kilometers up to Samkita were usually considered a journey of ten to twelve hours. As the boat was very heavily laden we had to allow a few more hours.

As we came out of the river branch into the principal stream, the day broke. About three hundred meters ahead near some huge sandbanks, I saw some dark lines moving in the water. At precisely that moment the paddlers stopped singing as if by command. The dark lines were hippopotamuses taking their morning bath. The natives are much afraid of them and always give them a wide berth, for the animals are unpredictable in their temper and have already destroyed many a boat.

A missionary formerly stationed in Lambarene used to make fun of the anxiety of his paddlers, and urge them to approach nearer the hippopotamuses. One day as he was just about to laugh at them again, the boat was flung into the air by a suddenly emerging hippopotamus, and only with difficulty were he and his crew able to save themselves. All his baggage was lost. Later he had the hole that the animal had made in the thick shell of the boat sawn out to keep as a souvenir. This incident, which occurred some few years ago, is told to every white man who urges his paddlers to go nearer the hippopotamuses.   [*Urwald*, pp. 39-40]

A Mangled Leg

Mrs. Faure, the wife of the missionary at N'Gomo, arrived this afternoon in the motorboat with a severe case of malaria. I had scarcely given her the first intramuscular injection of quinine, when a dugout brought a young man whose right thigh had been broken and the flesh frightfully lacerated by a hippopotamus in Lake Sonange. He was otherwise in bad shape as well.

Two men were going home from their fishing. As they approached the village landing place, a hippopotamus unexpectedly surfaced, throwing their boat into the air. The other man had escaped but this one had been in the water, chased by the angry beast, for half an hour. In spite of his broken thigh he was finally able to get to land. I was afraid that his wound would be badly infected, since during the twelve-hour boat ride the mangled leg had been wrapped in dirty rags.   [*Urwald*, pp. 54-55]

Who Is Responsible?

I found the young man who had been wounded by the hippopotamus in bad condition. My three weeks' absence had prevented my operating on him in time. I immediately amputated his leg, but he died during the operation.

As he was breathing his last, his brother began to cast threatening glances at the man who had been with him on the fateful fishing expedition, and had come with him to help care for him — speaking to him in a low voice. While the body was growing cold their language became excited. Joseph took me to one side and explained what was going on. N'Kendju, the companion, had gone with the unfortunate man on the fishing trip on which they were attacked by the hippopotamus; he indeed had extended the invitation to go. According to native law he was therefore responsible for him and liable to punishment. It was for this reason that he had already left his village and tarried all these weeks at the wounded man's side. And now that they were taking the dead man down the river to his village, he was expected to go along so that the case might be immediately settled. But he did not want to go, knowing it would mean death.

I explained to the brother that I considered N'Kendju my employee and that I would not let him go. An excited altercation immediately flared up between the two of us, while the dead man was being laid out in the dugout and the mother and the aunts were beginning their lamentations for the dead. He maintained that N'Kendju would not be put to death but would only be punished with a fine. Joseph, however, assured me that no reliance could be put upon such assurances. I had to remain on the shore until they had left, as they would otherwise have dragged the man secretly into the boat by force.   [*Urwald*, pp. 70-71]

A HIPPOPOTAMUS AND THE HOSPITAL ROOF

Where could I find the thirty people needed to repair the roof of my house? At the time we had in the hospital almost no one who was not very ill or wholly incapacitated. I decided to take a chance and on Sunday afternoon cross the river to the villages on the other side to see if I could find some people. I had little hope of success, for it was the season when all the men were at the lumbering areas in the forests. But there they were, back in the villages for a great palaver. When I found them, they were under a great tree listening to a black lawyer. Going from group to group, I persuaded some of them to come on Monday to help me with the roof.

Continuing on my way I stumbled upon Mr. Bochowiak's paddler, who was sitting there very gloomy. The preceding night a hippopotamus had overturned their boat when they were on the way to Lambarene. If the misfortune had not occurred close to a sandbank, they would all have been drowned, as they came from the interior and did not know how to swim. They had at the moment such a fear of the water and the hippopotamuses that it was not difficult for me to persuade them to work safely on my roof for one or two days, and at the same time earn a present. They had lost all of their belongings in the water through the accident.

[*Mitteilungen,* II, p. 54]

THE JUNGLE PEOPLE CRAVE MEAT

Since the water has remained high, the natives have not been able to undertake any great fishing expeditions. Nowhere now are supplies of smoked fish to be had, which usually for months at a time satisfy the need for meat. The Catholic mission which is usually well supplied with everything has been able to gather hardly five hundred small carp for its school children. The Father Superior, who is an excellent shot, goes out, therefore, hunting courageously for hippopotamuses. With twelve boys he travels for a whole day looking for these wild animals. That means spending a rainy night on a sandbank or in a swamp. Sometimes they have to return two or three weeks later without booty, but sometimes with the great dugout full to the point of sinking with smoked hippopotamus flesh. In that case the school work is assured for the winter. A Negro boy who gets meat two or three times in the week is willing and eager to learn; without meat he is a listless creature forever complaining of hunger even when he is stuffed full of rice. The jungle people have a really morbid craving for meat.   [*Mitteilungen,* I, p. 44]

AN INSTRUMENT OF TORTURE

One of the patients presented my wife with a hippopotamus whip. What is a hippopotamus whip? When a hippopotamus is killed, the hide, which is from one to two centimeters thick, is cut into strips about four centimeters wide and one and a half meters long.

Then each strip is wound into a spiral and stretched on a board. When it has dried, a dreadful instrument of torture, one and a half meters long, supple and sharp-cornered, is ready.

[*Urwald,* p. 64]

A HIPPOPOTAMUS BELOW THE GARDEN

For some months a hippopotamus has made his home in the river below our garden. From our house we can hear him at night breathing and trumpeting. Fortunately he has not yet taken a fancy to walk around in our garden beds with his little feet.

[*Lettres,* No. 4, p. 7]

A DEATH SENTENCE

As for the hippopotamus who is frequenting the hospital waters, I regret the necessity of making an unpleasant report about him. He is rude and malicious. Seized by a blind rage, he attacks approaching dugouts, capsizes them and pursues the occupants in the water. In this way he has killed a man and grievously wounded a woman inmate of the hospital. One moonlight night Dr. Goldschmid, Dr. Holm and I saw him hurl himself violently at a dugout, whose paddler did not suspect his presence and was just able, by a sudden turn, to avoid this attack. Since he has become dangerous to those who arrive in dugouts at the hospital or leave it during the night, his death sentence has been pronounced. But secretly we hope that the sentence will not have to be carried out and that the monster, warned by some premonition, will prefer to go off somewhere else to display his savagery and meanness.

[*Lettres,* No. 5, p. 6]

THE DISOBEDIENT BABY

On the return journey from Samkita we encountered a herd of fifteen hippopotamuses. A very young one played around on the sandbank after the rest of the herd had already plunged into the water, and would not obey its mother when she called to it anxiously.

[*Urwald,* p. 69]

STRANGELY BEAUTIFUL MOMENTS

I myself once had an encounter with a hippopotamus which fortunately turned out well.

One autumn day towards evening, I was called to visit a planter. To reach him we had to pass through a narrow canal — about fifty meters long — which had a rapid current. On the outward journey we saw two hippopotamuses in the distance. When we were about to return, the men at the store advised me, because night was coming on, to make about a two-hour detour to avoid the hippopotamuses and the narrow canal. But the paddlers were so tired that I did not have the heart to demand the extra exertion of them.

We had hardly reached the entrance to the canal when, thirty meters in front of us, two hippopotamuses emerged. Their roaring was like the sound children make when they blow into a watering can, but somewhat louder. The paddlers pressed close to the bank, where the current was weakest; the hippopotamuses accompanied us, swimming along the other bank. We proceeded centimeter by centimeter. It was wonderfully beautiful and exciting. In the middle of the stream a few palm trees that had taken root there rose out of the water, swaying like reeds. On the bank loomed a black wall of jungle. The magic of the moonlight fell on everything. The paddlers gasped, encouraging one another with low calls; the hippopotamuses, lifting their monstrous heads out of the water, glared angrily at us.

In a quarter of an hour we had gotten out of the canal and were traveling down the little branch of the stream, the hippopotamuses sending after us a parting roar. I vowed that never again in the future would I run that risk to save a detour of two hours. Still I should not like to lose the memory of those strangely beautiful moments.   [*Urwald,* pp. 54ff.]

6

Gorillas, Chimpanzees and Monkeys

THE ANTHROPOID APES

The so-called anthropoid apes — the chimpanzees and the gorillas — are not reckoned among the wild game. The most valiant hunter does not want to encounter them. Usually they attack immediately they are seen and have the hunter by the throat before he can make use of his gun. Human beings are no match for the strength of these apes when they are full-grown. Sometimes they are real monsters, two and a half meters high, and with powerful arms. The hand of a gorilla killed a few years ago in the vicinity of the middle Congo weighed five kilograms. Ordinarily these apes kill the hated man by biting him in the neck.

But there are instances of their leaving a man unmolested if he remains absolutely motionless. A white acquaintance who, with a caravan of bearers in the region north of Lambarene, was transporting rice, tobacco and salt, got tired one morning waiting for his bearers to load their burdens and went ahead of them on the forest path he knew so well. Suddenly at a bend in the trail he came upon a pair of gorillas holding a young one by the hand, as townspeople might take their child for a walk. There was no time to snatch his gun from his shoulder. In any case it would have been quite useless. There was nothing for the wanderer to do but stand at attention, as far as his trembling limbs would permit.

Father, mother and child stared at him steadily. After their first curiosity was satisfied, the young gorilla let go of its mother's hand to reach for the buttons on the white man's coat. While it played with them the white man smiled broadly at it so that it would not be frightened. Had he made a movement of fear the old gorilla would have immediately torn him to shreds. After this play had lasted for a little time the gorilla mother took the child again by the hand and drew it away from the white man, as if to say: "Now you have looked long enough at this freak." And father, mother and child went on their way. The white man, however, collapsed. Since that time he has never wandered ahead of his caravan in the early morning.

Another white man had built a field railway in his forest to bring out the wood. One day as he went out to visit a newly completed piece of the road, he met four chimpanzees who were sitting on the rails and apparently talking together about this new contrivance. They saw him coming but did not stir from the spot, glaring at him as if they wanted to call him to account for what he was doing to the forest. He did not dare go by, but postponed the inspection of the new line until the following day.

The district southwest of Lambarene is usually considered to be the part of equatorial Africa where most gorillas are to be found. Here the American professor, Garner, who died a few years ago, carried on his study of ape speech. He is said to have learned it by listening to gorillas. For days and nights he lived in the jungle in a strong cage, listening to them converse around the cage. In spite of the long article he wrote about the apes, I believe that he understood no more of their speech than any of the rest of us. While I was with him I got the impression that he was shamming.

The natives maintain that the gorillas live together in villages, and they do not dare enter the forests known to harbor these gorilla colonies. Two white men who were looking for a good place to cut wood came upon such a forest. The Negroes with them explained that they would not accompany them any farther.

"From the earliest days this wood has belonged to the gorillas, not to men," they said.

The whites laughed at them for believing such tales, and as the forest seemed to be rich in precious woods they decided to explore it themselves. For weapons they had with them only two light fowling-pieces. After they had wandered about for some distance unmolested they saw a gorilla, who withdrew immediately upon seeing them. A few minutes later a pair of gorillas suddenly appeared. These also withdrew, though a bit hesitantly. A few moments later the men found themselves face to face with a couple

of gorillas and a young one. By this time they began to think that there really was a gorilla colony there. Still, emboldened by the behavior of the gorillas they had already met, they unhesitatingly approached this new pair. The gorillas, indeed, drew back.

Suddenly, however, the male gorilla, a powerful brute, left its mate and child and rushed with growls and snarls at the whites. No escape was to be thought of. Fortunately one of them was an experienced hunter who knew how gorillas attack. The gorilla runs on all fours, supporting itself with its long forearms on the ground; a few meters from its victim it suddenly rises to its full height to seize him by the neck. Both men waited for this moment and at a distance of five meters planted their load of shot in the head of the gorilla. It fell, dead.

The men, however, ran back to their Negroes as fast as their feet would carry them and gave up once and for all their plan of clearing the timber from the forest of the gorilla towns.

[*Jagd,* pp. 1-3]

The Gorilla Lay in Wait

With us for a rather long time we had a native hunter whose hand had been torn by the frightful teeth of a gorilla. He had fired a shot at the animal, which he had suddenly met on the path, and considered himself fortunate when instead of attacking him it fled. The gorilla, however, lay in wait for him behind a tree, and when he was returning by the same path, there was a struggle in which the hunter very narrowly escaped death.　[*Mitteilungen,* III, p. 28]

An Enormous Gorilla

This summer we have had the very difficult case of a black hunter seriously injured by an enormous gorilla. He had wounded it with a rifle shot but then, being out of ammunition, had gone away without despatching it. Unknown to him, the gorilla had followed him home, catching up with him in the vicinity of his hut, where it jumped on him. The beast tossed the man about in the air like a ball, and made cruel wounds with its teeth all over his body. We had to keep the man under anesthetics for more than two hours while we were disinfecting and dressing his wounds, and months passed before the injured man could leave the hospital, his hand still maimed.   [*Lettres,* No. 11, p. 4]

THE GORILLA AND THE PAGNES

I have recently heard of a curious incident concerning a gorilla, an incident which took place in a forest logging camp, where the natives, under the direction of a white foreman, were cutting down okoumes. It happened that several times a powerful gorilla had rushed out at the native women who were carrying food to their husbands. Terrified, they had thrown to the ground the pots they were carrying and discarded their *pagnes*[1] so as to escape more quickly. The gorilla did not pursue them, but did justice to the food which had fallen to the ground, and carried off the pots and the clothes abandoned by the women. As these attacks by the gorilla who had taken a fancy to their menu were becoming more and more frequent, they decided to organize a hunt. The gorilla retreated to an enormous hollow tree trunk, where it was killed. It was discovered that the cavity in the trunk was filled with the pots, utensils and *pagnes* which the women had discarded in their flight.

[*Lettres,* No. 12, p. 2]

WILD BEASTS

In surgery during the past year we have had to deal particularly with people attacked by wild beasts or injured as a result of accidents in lumbering operations. We have succeeded in saving the lives of three persons badly mauled by gorillas, and of two others who had been surprised and seriously wounded by hippopotamuses. Doctor Meyländer had for his first operation in Africa a woman who had set her foot upon an alligator while she was fishing, taking it for a tree trunk lying in the mud. He skillfully sewed up the deep tears in the poor woman's muscles which the mistake had cost her. A man was brought to us with serious head wounds inflicted by a leopard; we could not save him.   [*Lettres,* No. 2, p. 4]

ATTACK FROM BEHIND

The wounds inflicted on the natives by savage beasts continually remind us that we are in the heart of the jungle. At this very moment

---

[1] A *pagne* is a large square of gaily printed cotton worn by the natives. [*Editor's note.*]

we have under treatment here a black patient who was attacked on a forest trail by a gorilla who pounced upon him from behind and tore off his scalp with its teeth and its nails before leaving him.

[*Lettres*, No. 13, p. 14]

CHIMPANZEES

A few weeks ago I had occasion to notice how close to the hospital are the beasts of the forest. As the natives had begun to make a plantation on some land belonging to the hospital, I had to fix the boundaries once again. Having laid off several hundred meters with the natives along the boundary line, I came upon numerous recent buffalo tracks in a clearing. And while I was having the boundary-line posts set, I heard my calls to the workmen followed each time by the cries of women and children.

"What's this?" I asked the workmen. "What are the women and children doing here?"

"Those women and children," they replied, laughing, "are the chimpanzees, who are vexed to hear your voice echoing here in the forest." [*Lettres*, No. 13, p. 14]

FIFI, THE BABY CHIMPANZEE

The very busy Miss Hausknecht seldom appears on the scene alone. Fifi, the baby chimpanzee, is always clinging to her apron. A year ago Fifi was brought to us when she was hardly more than a few days old. A native hunter had shot her mother. At the beginning Miss Hausknecht was afraid of the terribly ugly creature, and did not dare touch her. But sympathy triumphed over all esthetic inhibitions. Fifi has now gotten over her teething and is already able to eat with a spoon, unassisted.

For some time Fifi has had a playmate in a somewhat older chimpanzee baby, which a European turned over to us when he went back to Europe, knowing that it would be in good hands.

[*Mitteilungen*, III, pp. 39-40]

AN INSEPARABLE COMPANION

Every morning a little tame monkey which I gave to Mrs. Russell upon her arrival goes into the forest with her as her inseparable companion. Even though it takes a walk up in the trees, it nonetheless comes back loyally to its mistress. [*Mitteilungen*, III, p. 50]

THE BEST GAME ANIMAL

The best game animal here is the monkey. He feels so secure high up in the tree that he indulges his natural curiosity and sticks to his place even when the hunter below takes aim at him. He is often a very easy mark, because he screams down angrily from the tree, grimacing meanwhile. A year ago a certain kind of black monkey was being trapped for its fur, which had become fashionable in Paris. A Syrian trader who was traveling along the African coast to buy these furs told me that it was the only deep black fur that did not have to be dyed. Now the fur has gone out of fashion and the black monkeys can rest in peace.   [*Jagd*, p. 1]

7

Leopards — and Leopard Men

A Marauding Leopard

For weeks a leopard has made the country around the mission station unsafe. One of the mission goats, grazing with its young one not far from our house, fell victim to it in broad daylight.

[*Mitteilungen*, II, p. 29]

The Leopard Wants Blood

On the return from Talagouga we stayed for two days in Samkita at the home of Mr. and Mrs. Morel, Alsatian missionaries.

Samkita is a place of leopards. One night last autumn one of these marauders broke into Mrs. Morel's hen house. When her prized hens began to cry out, her husband hurried off to get someone to help, while she kept watch in the darkness. They thought a native had broken in to get a hen to roast. On hearing a noise on the roof, Mrs. Morel went nearer the hen house to identify the thief, if possible. But with one mighty leap he had already disappeared into the darkness.

When they opened the door twenty-two hens lay dead on the ground, their breasts torn open. Only the leopard kills in this way, for his first desire is to get blood to drink. His victims were taken away. One of them was filled with strychnine and left lying before the door. Two hours later the leopard came back and devoured it. While the leopard was writhing in convulsions it was shot by Mr. Morel.

A short time before our arrival another leopard had appeared at Samkita and had torn a number of goats to pieces

[*Urwald*, p. 68]

INFECTION FROM LEOPARDS

Every morning these days when the time comes for bandaging, the "leopard man" is called up. He is a quiet young man who was attacked by a leopard while asleep in his hut. The leopard struck him with his paw on the upper right arm, and ran off as people were hurrying up with a light. As the Negroes know from experience the frightful infection that comes with a wound from leopards' claws, they immediately put the injured man in a dugout to bring him to me.

When they arrived twelve hours later, the upper arm was already badly swollen and extremely painful. Moreover, fever had begun to set in. No sign of injury could be plainly made out, except four tiny punctures like those made by needles. When an opening was made with the knife it could be seen that the claws had torn the flesh down to the bone.

Our leopard man will soon be able to leave. He makes himself useful by helping with the ironing.   [*Mitteilungen,* I, pp. 42-43]

A WOUNDED LEOPARD

The most dangerous thing of all is to pursue a wounded leopard. Because he forgot to be cautious, an Italian lumber exploiter recently found himself in a very dangerous situation. While wandering through some grassland southwest of Cape Lopez he unexpectedly came upon a leopard which he shot and, as the blood tracks revealed, seriously wounded. After a little search he found the leopard in a depression grown up to sedge. At the very moment when he was once more in a position to shoot at it, his Negroes whom he had left behind also caught sight of the leopard and let out a loud cry to warn their master. This so angered the leopard that it sprang upon the white man with the last ounce of its strength. Unable to shoot, he stretched out the butt end of his gun, hoping that the leopard would sink its teeth into it; and this the animal did, as the holes in the wood still show.

Then step by step the Italian retreated, parrying the claws of the leopard with the butt of his gun — just like a fencer — to give his people time to hurry up with their spears. Unfortunately he stumbled and fell. Immediately the leopard seized his arm in its

jaws, tearing the flesh to the bone in its death struggle with the Negroes' spears. When the Italian was brought to me after a journey of several days it was doubtful whether the arm could be saved. After seven weeks of treatment I was able to let him go cured. But how he had suffered when we dressed his deeply infected wound!

A few months before, I had tended a Negro who had been clawed by a leopard in his hut during the night.

The leopard has a preference for dogs. One carried two dogs out of a lumber exploiter's house in broad daylight. If no dogs are available, it contents itself with hens. When it has discovered a hen house, it leaves nothing alive even if it is being fired at. If it is frightened away, it will be back in half an hour. This boldness usually costs its life.   [*Jagd*, pp. 8-9]

HUMAN LEOPARDS

At the ship's table, after the price of lumber and the question of labor have been discussed, the conversation turns to the bands of "human leopards," whose excesses have greatly increased everywhere in recent years, spreading over the entire west coast of Africa. The Duala missionaries told me that they visit neighborhoods so terrorized by leopard men that for months no one dares leave his hut after nightfall. Two years ago one of the leopard men committed a murder at the Lambarene mission station.

"Leopard men" are men with the delusion that they are really leopards and have a compulsion to kill human beings. They try in their killing to behave like leopards. They go on all fours; they bind leopard claws or iron claws on their hands and feet, to leave behind them tracks like those made by leopards; and they tear the arteries in the necks of their victims as the leopard does.

The extraordinary and sinister fact is that most of them have become leopard men quite involuntarily. They have been made members of the company of human leopards without their knowledge. A magic potion has been prepared in a human skull from the blood of a murdered man. A person secretly chosen in advance gets some of this mixed in his drink. When he has drunk he is informed that he has partaken of the magic potion and henceforth belongs to the brotherhood. No one rebels. The belief that a magic

drink possesses a power that no one can escape dominates them all.
Automatically they obey. The next step is usually to compel them
to lead a brother or sister to some place where he or she may be
attacked and killed by the leopard men. After that they themselves
are obliged to kill.

An official in the interior of the Ogowe district who recently
received an order to put an end to the misdeeds of the leopard men
arrested ninety suspicious characters. They would betray nothing,
however, but instead poisoned each other in prison.

How far the bands of leopard men represent a wave of pure
superstition, and how far desires for revenge and plunder have
subsequently become involved, cannot be determined. Along with
other secret associations they are a manifestation of a sinister
process of fermentation in Africa. Newly reviving superstition,
primitive fanaticism, and a very modern bolshevism are today
forming the most extraordinary combinations in the black regions
of the earth.   [*Mitteilungen,* I, pp. 18-19]

LEOPARDS WITHOUT FUR

In a Bavoumbo village the chief assigned us as a shelter a house
appearing from the outside quite spacious, but containing rooms
which were astonishingly low. When we examined it we discovered
that the big house was only a shell covering two smaller ones. The
primitives do not like big rooms. We have seen houses where one
could enter only by stooping and where one could not remain
except by crouching or lying down. The government compels the
blacks to build larger houses. But a small hut is easier to heat,
and the primitive who has few clothes is afraid of the night chill,
particularly in the mountains. For this reason he sets up in the
big house, which regulation compels him to construct, a little house
complete with its own roof, window and door. The inner hut constitutes the real shelter; the other is there to keep up appearances
with the authorities.

Of course we put our beds in the corridor between the two inside
huts. The chief tried to dissuade us from doing this, pretending
that there was in the vicinity a "tiger" which attacked people. We
would not let ourselves be shut up tightly and we promised him that
we would keep a big fire going all night to keep wild beasts off.

That did not satisfy him. He brought us great nets made of strong cords, which he stretched carefully around the whole house, taking great care that no hole was there to let the "tiger" through. In front of the entrance he stretched the net double and hung a little bell there that would ring the moment anyone touched the net.

Thinking that the country must be particularly rich in leopards we expressed the desire to buy one of the skins. But Zengui, one of our most faithful porters, said to us in the chief's presence: "These leopards have no fur. What they fear here are not leopards, but men who are like leopards." Such leopard men form secret societies with vast ramifications, whose chiefs tell them which people to kill. The attitude of our men revealed to me how unsafe the district of the Bavoumbos was. Ordinarily they march in a rather broken line, some far ahead and others dallying in the rear; here they march one directly behind the other.   [*Lettres*, No. 3, pp. 8-9] [1]

THE WORST BITE

Two natives, both of whom have been bitten by men, are with us. One of them got bitten while he was trying to arrest a delinquent debtor. Biting as a means of defense is more common among the blacks than among us.

"The worst bite," says Joseph, "is that of the leopard; worse still is the bite of the poisonous snake; still worse is the monkey's bite; the worst of all, however, is that of a man."

There is some truth in this. Up till now I have seen in Africa about twelve wounds caused by the human bite. All of them showed immediate symptoms of serious infection. In two cases there developed the danger of general blood poisoning, although the patients came to me within a few hours. One of the two who have just now come with human bites will have to have the last joint of a finger removed. His name is Vendakambano; he is a joiner. I made him promise that after he was healed he would stay with me two months to help with the building — a promise he made with fervor.   [*Mitteilungen*, II, pp. 32-33]

---

[1] Although this letter was written by Miss Emma Hausknecht, one of the Lambarene nurses, it is included in this series of Doctor Schweitzer's letters. [*Editor's note.*]

8

Josephine, the Tame Wild Boar

One day a Negro woman brought me a tame wild boar about two months old.

"It is called Josephine, and it will follow you around like a dog," she said.

We agreed upon five francs as the price. My wife was just then away for a few days. With the help of Joseph and N'Kendju, my hospital assistant, I immediately drove some stakes into the ground and made a pen, with the wire netting rather deep in the earth. Both of my black helpers smiled.

"A wild boar will not remain in a pen; it digs his way out from under it," said Joseph.

"Well, I should like to see this little wild boar get under this wire netting sunk deep in the earth," I answered.

"You will see," said Joseph.

The next morning the animal had already gotten out. I felt almost relieved about it, for I had promised my wife that I would make no new acquisition to our zoo without her consent, and I had a foreboding that a wild boar would not, perhaps, be to her liking.

When I came up from the hospital for the midday meal, however, there was Josephine waiting for me in front of the house, and looking at me as if she wanted to say: "I will remain ever so faithful to you, but you must not repeat the trick with the pen." And so it was.

When my wife arrived she shrugged her shoulders. She never enjoyed Josephine's confidence and never sought it. Josephine had a very delicate sensibility about such things. In time, when she had come to understand that she was not permitted to go up on the

114

veranda, things became bearable. On a Saturday some weeks later, however, Josephine disappeared. In the evening the missionary met me in front of my house and shared my sorrow, since Josephine had also shown some attachment to him.

"I feel sure she has met her end in some Negro's pot," he said. "It was inevitable."

With the blacks a wild boar, even when tamed, does not fall within the category of a domestic animal but remains a wild animal that belongs to him who kills it. While he was still speaking, however, Josephine appeared, behind her a Negro with a gun.

"I was standing," he said, "in the clearing, where the ruins of the former American missionary's house are still to be seen, when I saw this wild boar. I was just taking aim, but it came running up to me and rubbed against my legs. An extraordinary wild boar! But imagine what it then did. It trotted away with me after it, and now here we are. So it's your wild boar? How fortunate that this did not happen to a hunter who is not so quick-witted as I." I understood this hint, complimented him generously and gave him a nice present.

But the thought that my wild boar was in constant danger, as the missionary had told me, troubled me, while the two of us were rubbing the back of the newly recovered animal with our feet, something which Josephine greatly loved.

"Listen, doctor," the missionary began suddenly, "tomorrow I have to preach, and as it will soon be necessary to touch upon the sin of theft in every service for our Negroes, I will bring in Josephine right off tomorrow morning as an illustration of the fact that an animal once wild and anybody's property nonetheless may afterwards become private property and inviolable, when it is cherished by someone."

I thanked him in advance for coming to my assistance with his choice of this significant example.

The next morning, in the second half of the sermon, Josephine was introduced. With rapt attention the Negroes listened as the missionary explained the complicated case and broadened the horizon of their notion of property. At that very moment — it made me almost ill — Josephine took her place beside the preacher! In Lambarene, you know, we have no chancel. The service of worship takes place in the corrugated-iron barrack in which the school is also held. The preacher stands on the ground. The doors are always left open, so that some air can come in. People are quite accustomed to have hens and sheep come and go during the service. The missionary's dogs regularly take part in it. I always took it for granted that my dog Caramba would go with me to the service. Whenever he heard the bell and the singing he could not be kept in the house. And if he had been tied up at that time he would have disturbed the discourse far more with his howling, which could be heard all over the mission station, than with his silent presence.

But that Josephine should also have become religious seemed horrible to me. Moreover, I was soon made forcibly aware that she did not know how to behave. She had come fresh from the marsh, covered with black mire. And now she walked among the benches, where the children sat, while they drew their knees up under their chins! Then she came to the women! Then to the other missionary! Then to the ladies of the mission with their white skirts, trying to rub herself against them! Then to the lady doctor! Then to me! At that moment she received a kick, the first she ever had from me. It was, however, justified.

I was not able to discourage Josephine's delight in the church service. She could not be shut up; neither could she be tied up, for she worked her way out of every harness that I contrived for her. The moment the bell sounded she ran to church. I do not think she missed any of the morning or evening prayers for the children. I proposed to the missionary who was in charge of the station that because of all this I should kill her. But he forbade me to do so: the animal should not lose her life because of such an instinct. In time Josephine began to behave more properly in church.

How shall I sufficiently praise your wisdom, Josephine! To avoid being bothered by gnats at night, you adopted the custom of wandering into the boy's dormitory, and of lying down there under the first good mosquito net. How many times because of this have I had to compensate, with tobacco leaves, those upon whom you forced yourself as a sleeping companion. And when the sand-fleas had so grown in your feet that you could no longer walk, you hobbled down to the hospital, let yourself be turned over on your back, endured the knife that the tormentors stuck into your feet, put up with the burning of the tincture of iodine, with which the wounds were daubed, and grunted your sincere thanks when the matter was once and for all done with!

"When a wild boar is more than six months old, it begins to eat hens," said N'Kendju.

"Josephine will not go so far as to eat hens," I replied with an unsteady voice.

"She will eat hens, for she is a wild boar," came the response with its inexorable logic. Nonetheless, I ventured to hope.

A Negro came and told me one of his hens was missing. I knew what he meant by this, gave him a gift and told him to be silent.

The lady missionary told me that one of her hens was missing. I knew what she meant by it. But I betrayed nothing, and simply said: "Yes, it is a bad business with the snakes around here." So I forced myself to believe in the innocence of Josephine.

One morning, however, as I was examining the blood of some patients under the microscope in the hospital, I heard the cackling of hens and through it all the voices of men calling. Shortly thereafter the boy Akaja appeared with a note from the lady doctor. The writing said: "Josephine has gotten in among the chickens, has eaten three of them, and has torn off the tail of the clucking hen. I saw it with my own eyes. You know what you have to do."

I knew it and did it. Josephine was enticed into the hospital, tied up, and expeditiously and artistically slaughtered. Before noon sounded her life came to an end. I estimate that she was about eight months old.

The bacon was cut into strips and stuck on little sticks which I carefully smoked and dried and put away hermetically sealed in a tin.

Not long after an official came to consult me, and I entertained him at lunch. He got some of the bacon.

"What? Smoked bacon? A rarity in this land."

"Sir, it comes from a tame wild boar. I had to kill it because it was eating hens."

"You had a tame wild boar? I had one also which I brought up with a nursing bottle. It cost me many a tin of Swiss milk. But it ran after me like a dog. Unfortunately it was stolen from me. I had given it the name of Josephine."

"In that case, my dear sir, you are now eating the bacon of the tame wild boar that you brought up on the nursing bottle. The woman who sold it to me had stolen it from you."   [*Josephine*]

9

Termites, Traveler Ants and Other Insects

TERMITES EVERYWHERE

The termites remind us constantly that our hospital is located in the virgin forest. We discover them now in the pharmacy shelves, now in the bandages, now in the beams of the buildings, now in the papers stacked up somewhere. What a ceaseless source of trouble! Especially since we do not always discover them before they have done considerable damage. Then we have to remove everything to find out where they have come in.

These injurious insects give us a great deal of work. Because of them I have to transfer all the medicines that come to me in cartons into well-sealed tin boxes. The insecticides now in use against the termites give hardly noticeable results. Recently we have tried D.D.T., a compound discovered in Strassburg in 1872 and then forgotten. Since 1941 it has again come into use.

[*Lettres*, No. 13, p. 14]

TERMITES, WEEVILS AND SCORPIONS

I was hoping to have a little rest. But I discovered that in spite of all precautions the termites had gotten into the boxes where the reserves of medicines and bandages were kept. So we had to open and unpack the many cases. The work demanded all our free time again for weeks. Fortunately I had discovered it in good time; otherwise the harm would have been much greater. The peculiar, delicate smell as of burning, which the termites cause, had warned me. There was no sign of them on the outside of the boxes. The invasion had occurred through a tiny hole in the floor. From the

121

first box they had eaten their way through to the boxes above and beside it. Apparently they had been attracted by a bottle of medicinal syrup, whose cork stopper had gotten loose.

Oh, the fight in Africa against creeping insects! How much time one loses with all the precautions to be taken! And with what helpless rage one must admit time and again that nonetheless he has been worsted.

My wife learned how to solder, so as to seal up the flour and maize in tins. But it happens that the frightful little weevils (*Chalandra granaria*) sometimes swarm by the thousands in the soldered tins. In a short time they turn the maize for the hens into dust.

Very much dreaded here are certain tiny scorpions and other stinging insects. One becomes so cautious that he never, as in Europe, puts his hand blindly into a drawer or a box. Only under the eye's watchful care does the hand dare proceed.

[*Urwald*, pp. 136ff.]

Termites and Firewood

Recently the termites got into a box that stood on the veranda of my house. I emptied it, broke it up, and gave the pieces to the Negro who helped me.

"You see, the termites are in it," I said. "You mustn't put this wood with the other firewood under the hospital, or the termites will get into the framework of the barracks. Go to the river and throw it into the water. Do you understand?"

"Yes, yes, don't worry," he replied.

It was evening. I was too tired to go down the hill again, and therefore was inclined to make an exception and trust a black man — this one was on the whole not a bad one. At ten o'clock, however, I became so uneasy that I took the lantern and went down to the hospital. The wood infested with the termites lay in the midst of the firewood. To save himself the ten meters to the river, the Negro had jeopardized my buildings!   [*Urwald*, pp. 129-30]

Traveler Ants

Serious enemies are the notorious traveler ants, which belong to the genus *Dorylus*. We suffer a great deal from them. In their great migrations they travel five or six abreast in perfectly ordered columns. I once observed, near my house, a column that took thirty-six hours to pass! If their course is over open ground or across a path, the warriors with their powerful jaws line up several rows deep on each side and protect the procession in which the ordinary traveler ants carry their young along. When they form protecting lanes they turn their backs to the procession like Cossacks guarding the Czar. In that position they remain for hours.

Usually three or four independent columns march along one beside the other but from five to fifty meters apart. At a particular moment they disperse. How the command is given we do not know. But in a trice a huge area is covered with a black swarm. Every living thing found on it is doomed. Even the great spiders on the trees cannot escape, for the frightful ravagers creep after them in droves up to the highest twig. And if in despair the spiders jump down from the tree, they fall victim to the ants on the ground. The spectacle is gruesome. The militarism of the jungle almost bears comparison with that in Europe.

Our house lies on one of the great military routes of the traveler ants. Usually they swarm at night. A scratching and a peculiar clucking of the hens warn us of the danger. Now no time must be lost. I spring out of bed, run to the hen house and open it. Hardly have I opened the door when the hens rush out; shut in they would be the victims of the ants. The latter creep into the nose and mouth of the hens until they are stifled. Then they devour them until in a short time only the white bones remain. Ordinarily it is the chickens that fall victim to the ravagers; the hens are able to defend themselves until help arrives.

Meanwhile my wife snatches the horn from the wall and blows it three times. This is the signal for N'Kendju, helped by the active men in the hospital, to bring buckets of water from the river. The water is mixed with lysol, and the ground around and under the house sprinkled with it.

While this is going on we are badly mistreated by the warriors. They creep up on us and take bites out of us. I once counted almost fifty on my body. The animals bite so firmly with their jaws that one cannot pull them off. If one pulls at them, the body is torn off, the jaws remaining in the flesh, and these must be detached separately. The whole drama is enacted in the darkness of the night by the light of the lantern held by my wife.

At last the ants move on. They cannot stand the smell of the lysol. Thousands of corpses lie in the puddles.

Once in the course of a single week we were attacked by them three times. Mr. Coillard, the missionary, whose memoirs I am now reading, likewise suffered a great deal in Zambesi from the traveler ant.

The principal migrations of the ants take place at the beginning and at the end of the rainy season. In the interval there is less reason to expect their attacks. In size these ants are not much bigger than our red European ants. But their jaws are much more strongly developed and they travel much faster. The remarkably rapid movement of all the African ants has impressed me particularly.   [*Urwald*, pp. 137ff.]

SPIDERS AND COCKROACHES

We hardly had time to unpack the most necessary things when night fell, as it always does here just after six o'clock. The bell called the children to evening devotions in the school hall. A host of crickets began to chirp, accompanying the chorale that drifted over to us. I sat on a trunk and listened, deeply stirred. At that moment a hateful shadow crept down the wall. I looked up in alarm and saw a huge spider. It was much bigger than the most magnificent ones I had seen in Europe. After an exciting hunt it was killed.

After supper at the Christols the school children appeared in front of the veranda, which was decorated with real Chinese lanterns, and sang in two parts some verses composed by the missionary Ellenberger to the tune of a Swiss folk song. We were escorted with lanterns up the path which runs along the hill to our house. But before we could think of sleep another fight had to be waged with spiders and great flying cockroaches, who regard the long-uninhabited house as their own property.   [*Urwald*, pp. 26-27]

THE SANDFLEA

Many sores are caused by the sandflea (*Rynchoprion penetrans*), which is much smaller than the common flea. The little female

The traveler ants proceed in columns two or three miles long through the jungle. Where they have to cross a path, they build a sort of tunnel like this, through which the marching myriads pass. On each side of the tunnel the warrior ants stand facing outward. ready to attack viciously anything that threatens the migrants. At a given signal all the ants scatter to feed; and then all vegetation and most animal life in the vicinity quickly disappear before their voracity. Even men have been killed by the ants.

bores into the most tender part of the toe, preferably under the nail, and a lump the size of a small lentil develops under the skin. The removal of the parasite causes a small wound. If dirt infects it, a kind of gangrene sets in, which often causes the loss of a joint or even the whole toe. Negroes with all ten toes intact are almost more difficult to find than those who have one or more mutilated ones.

It is an interesting fact that the sandflea, which now constitutes a real plague in Central Africa, was not indigenous here but was brought in from South America as late as 1872. In a single decade it had spread all over the Dark Continent from the Atlantic to the Pacific. One of the worst ants that we have here, the so-called "sangunagenta," also came over the ocean from South America in chests, and it is now domesticated.   [*Urwald,* pp. 83-84]

INSECT PESTS

What the timber workers have to suffer in the day from the tsetse, and at night from the mosquito, cannot be described. All day long, moreover, they have to stand up to their hips in swamps. All of them often have fever and rheumatism.   [*Urwald,* p. 95]

THE SLY TSETSE

At sunrise the tsetse flies appear. They fly only by day. Compared with them the worst mosquitoes are harmless creatures. The tsetse is about one and a half times as big as our common housefly, which it resembles externally, except that its wings do not lie parallel with each other, but overlap like two scissor-blades.

To get blood the tsetse will penetrate the thickest cloth. At the same time it is very cautious and sly and skillfully avoids the slapping hand. The moment the body on which it has lighted makes the slightest movement it flies off and hides.

Its flight is silent. One can protect himself to a certain extent with small fly-swatters. Cautious as the tsetse is, it avoids settling on a light background, on which it would be very visible. Therefore white clothes are the best protection against it.

I found this fact perfectly established on our journey. Two of us wore white clothes, the third yellow. The two hardly had a single tsetse; the third was continually plagued. The blacks were the worst sufferers.   [*Urwald*, p. 41]

Tsetses and Mosquitoes

Sleeping sickness is usually carried by the *Glossina palpalis*, a kind of tsetse fly. If the tsetse has once been infected by someone who has sleeping sickness, it can spread the disease for a long time, perhaps for its entire life span. The trypanosomes which are ingested with the blood of the sick man live and increase and pass through the saliva into the blood of the men whom it subsequently bites. The *Glossina* flies only by day.

A closer study of sleeping sickness reveals that it can also be carried by mosquitoes, if they satisfy their hunger on a healthy person immediately after they have stung someone with sleeping sickness and so have trypanosomes in the saliva. The host of mosquitoes, therefore, continues by night the work that the *Glossina* carries on by day. Poor Africa!   [*Urwald*, pp. 79-80]

10

Domestic Animals

JADED HORSES AND MULES

At Dakar, the great port of the Senegal colony, my wife and I set foot for the first time on the soil of Africa, to which we intended to consecrate our lives. It gave us a solemn feeling.

I shall cherish no kindly memory of Dakar, for I cannot help recalling the cruelty toward animals shown there. The city lies on a steep slope, and the streets are partly in very bad condition still. The lot of the poor draught animals at the mercy of the Negroes is frightful. I have nowhere else seen such jaded horses and mules. Once when I came upon two Negroes riding on a cart heavily laden with wood, stuck in the broken stones of a newly laid street, and found them striking and screaming at the poor animal, I could not proceed on my way; I forced them to get off and push with me until the three of us had freed the wagon. They were much astonished, but obeyed without opposition.

"If you cannot stand by and see animals mistreated, then don't go to Africa," said the lieutenant to me on the way back. "You will see many horrible things of this kind here."   [*Urwald,* pp. 15-16]

OUR HERD OF GOATS

So that we need not always, at a very high price, import all our milk from Switzerland, we are trying to bring up a herd of goats. These goats running wild give hardly half a glass of milk a day, but we hope in time to improve the breed.   [*Mitteilungen,* III, p. 39]

THE PROBLEM OF MILK

Our goats give us now about one-fifth of the milk we need for the hospital and the household. How much trouble they cause because of the itching that ceaselessly torments them! I used to cherish the hope that the natives would little by little come to raise milk goats in their villages. But the goats are a prey to a skin disease, and now I know the trouble and the meticulous care necessary to keep them from dying of it. I begin to question whether our natives will ever be capable of raising the milk producers which the country so much needs. As for the raising of cows, it is not to be thought of, because of the tsetse fly.   [*Lettres,* No. 4, p. 7]

GOATS ARE DESTRUCTIVE

The direction of everything which does not, properly speaking, belong to the medical service is the responsibility of Miss Emma Hausknecht, who has again been back in Africa since the month of July 1935. She has complete charge of the kitchen and household, the poultry yard and the stable for the goats. She also looks out for the maintenance of the buildings and the small boats. She has had quite a number of houses whitewashed — no mean task — and has replaced with posts of reinforced concrete a good many of the hardwood piles on which our buildings were resting.

An epizootic disease that has ravaged our poultry yard has caused her some uneasiness. She also has a good deal of difficulty in reconciling the raising of goats with the protection of the plantation. Both are indispensable to us: the goats to give us the milk with which we feed our little black orphans and the fruits of the plantation to improve the food rations for the sick. In the tropical heat it is impossible to keep the goats in their stable; we must let them run free all day long in the plantation. But, although they might have plenty of excellent grass, they attack the leaves of the small fruit trees or the tender shoots of the palm tree. As for the fruit trees whose leaves they disdain, they help themselves to their bark. We therefore have to enclose all the young trees with wire netting and barbed wire.

This would be perfect if it were not for the native women staying at the hospital. These women, instead of going to the forest to get their supply of firewood, think it more convenient to pull up, during the night, the stakes that hold up the netting and the barbed wire, and to use them as wood to make their pots boil. So almost every

These goats, lined up on the logs, watch the photographer curiously. In a country where cattle have been unable to live because of the tsetse fly, these goats are prized for their milk and their meat.

morning the goats find young trees undefended against their destructive impulses.   [*Lettres,* No. 9, p. 3]

THREE HUNDRED FRANCS AND A GOAT

During the whole week the wounded man lay in the hospital, I kept the boy who had fired the shot at him beside me, so that the victim's relatives should do him no harm nor carry him off to extort a huge fine from him. Ordered to assist in the kitchen and with the washing, the boy began to help Miss Kottmann.

At last, to my joy, I was able to bring about a reconciliation between the wounded man and the one who shot him. The boy paid three hundred francs in monthly installments of fifty francs, adding a goat as well. Some living thing must be given in every case involving an offense against a man's life. Had he lost his arm, the boy would have had to buy him a wife.   [*Mitteilungen,* II, p. 21]

FOR THE BENEFIT OF THE COOKING POT

In the course of the second operation I was performing with Dr. Lauterberg, one of the natives surprised us by rushing into the room with the cry: "They are killing the doctor's hens."

"They" were the Bendjabi,[1] who can as yet only creep, and his comrade. It would have astonished me, if they had not taken advantage of the time when the doctors and orderlies were all engaged indoors for the benefit of their cooking pot!

[*Mitteilungen,* II, pp. 37-38]

METHYLVIOLET HENS

Of course, my hens are no more safe than those of the missionary from the Bendjabis. Indeed a good many of them have already ended up in their kettles and provided an evening's banquet. If we are fortunate in catching the culprit, we paint a hen on his forehead, one on each cheek, one on his breast, and one on his back, with methylviolet. So decorated, he is taken with us on all excursions, and with proper explanation shown to people. This seems to be somewhat successful.   [*Mitteilungen,* II, p. 18]

---

[1] A thieving member of a native tribe. [*Editor's note.*]

THE PORCELAIN EGG

The whites here have introduced the custom of putting porcelain eggs in the nests of the hens to fool them, as far as possible, when the eggs they lay are taken away from them every day. However, it happens that not only the hens, for whom this is intended, but also others interested in the eggs are fooled.

Before I came here, the following incident took place. A missionary from the mission station of Lambarene was going off one morning before daylight on a preaching trip. Wishing to take along with him as provisions for the journey some newly laid eggs, he opened the little door through which the hens passed, groping blindly with his hand for the nest. Then something extraordinary happened. His hand struck something cold and smooth in the hen house, swinging to and fro.

Hastily he got a lantern and the door key. When the door was opened and the light thrown cautiously into the room, he saw that the pendulum was a snake two meters long, from whose jaws the porcelain egg protruded. It had forced its way in through a hole in the roof and was hanging over the nest. It had easily swallowed the hen's eggs — but it had been unable to crush this one as it had the others. On the contrary, the porcelain egg had stuck in its throat and it could neither get it down nor throw it up. Helplessly it capitulated to the death blow, a victim to the white man's trick.

In the same hen house my wife later placed the porcelain egg in the nest of her precious hens. As both of the small house-boys were fond of eggs, they often used to steal the contents of the nest. Once they carelessly did so thorough a job of it that all the eggs, including the porcelain one, were missing. In this way their crime came to light. Of course, they swore solemnly that they had taken nothing away, and that it was all caused by the carelessness of the hens.

In the course of the morning one of the boys, radiant, came running to my wife. The hens were beginning to lay again, he said, and even the big gray hen that had come from Europe had gotten off her nest and left a huge egg lying in it. It was the porcelain egg, which the culprits had brought back again. Since they had been able neither to break nor to boil this egg with its hard shell, they

One of the natives goes into the jungle each day to gather fresh leaves for the antelopes that live in pens beside the Doctor's house. But the goats and the African sheep that roam freely about the hospital think they should have some also.

concluded that it came from the European hen and that only the whites knew how to cook it.

A few years ago Upsi, the sly monkey who always stole eggs and never let himself get caught at it, fell a victim to this trick. Early one morning I found him, with a troubled expression on his face, sitting on a post of the poultry-yard enclosure holding an egg in his hand. He did not spring away but remained sitting there, as if he wanted to call me to witness the incomprehensible thing which puzzled him. He struck the egg against the post, but it did not break. He rolled it between his hands but could not crush it. It made no difference when he hit it harder. pressed it more vigorously between his hands, and even tried to use his teeth.

He remained quiet for a moment, to gather new strength, looking at me as if to ask if I at all understood this thing. It seemed to me that I would have to burst into laughter — although this is something one should avoid before an excited monkey, for it makes him fly into a still greater passion and under certain circumstances makes him aggressive. Then it came to him that his misfortune could once again be attributed to the infamy of man.

He made his anger known to me by grimacing fiercely and baring his teeth. After an interval of giving vent to his rage at the unlucky thing, he threw it into the court, spit at me and sprang away. For several days I had the impression that he was avoiding me because I had been the witness of his discomfiture.

[*Geschichten,* pp. 76ff.]

11

Creatures of the Deep

Shining Jellyfish

Wonderful in the evening is the glimmer of the sea as the ship ploughs along. The foam is phosphorescent and the jellyfish rise in it, giving off light like shining globes.

[*Urwald,* p. 19]

Hyenas of the Deep

"A shark! A shark!"

I rushed out of the writing room and was shown a black triangle sticking out of the water some fifty meters from the ship, and moving in our direction. It was the fin of the dread monster.

Whoever has once seen it never forgets it and never confuses it with anything else. The harbors of West Africa swarm with sharks. At Kotonou I saw one, attracted by the kitchen refuse, come within ten meters of the ship. As the light was good and the water transparent, I could for several minutes see the whole gray and yellow length of its glistening body and observe how it turned halfway over so as to get into its mouth, which we all know lies on the underside of the head, whatever seemed attractive to it.

Despite the sharks, the Negroes in all of these ports dive for coins. Accidents seldom happen, because the noise they make at the time gets on the nerves of even these hyenas of the deep. At Tabou I was surprised to see one of the diving Negroes remain quite silent while others were crying out for more coins. Later I noticed that he was the most skillful of them all, and had to remain silent because he was using his mouth as a purse and could hardly close it any more because of the *sous* and *groschen* in it.

[*Urwald,* pp. 16-17]

ELECTRIC FISH

In July we were plunged into deep sorrow by the death of Mr. Abrezol, the missionary who had just arrived. One morning at sunrise, while bathing in a lake near N'Gomo, he was drowned before the eyes of Noel and Mr. Hermann, another missionary, with whom he had gone on a journey of several days' duration. His body was found, but it could not be brought to Lambarene as the motorboat had been damaged by grounding on a sandbank. So he was buried on the hill at N'Gomo. He was a lovable and unusually capable man who had won all our hearts.

Since several people have been drowned in this same lake in a very mysterious fashion, we assume that they have been stung and paralyzed by an electric fish.   [*Mitteilungen*, I, pp. 40-41]

AN INFECTED FISH BITE

Dr. Nessman and Dr. Lauterberg were greatly pleased because a woman who had been bitten by a fish and had come to them with a severely infected arm asked to have the arm amputated. She came from the district where the Bendjabi upon whom we had operated had preached to the people the value of an amputation. She, too, recovered.   [*Mitteilungen*, II, p. 49]

WHALE FISHERIES

At Cape Lopez on the sea, the whale fisheries have recently had a great revival. At the beginning of June the whales come north to the equator from the southern ocean. They are looking for warmer waters, for in the southern hemisphere at this season winter is setting in. The vicinity of Cape Lopez teems with fish and is a favorite resort for them. Here, from June until October, the Norwegian whalers hunt them.

The whale fishing is carried on today with very modern equipment by two small Norwegian cities. Speedy little steamers are provided with cannons shooting big, heavy, four-pronged harpoons that kill the animal at once. These little steamers travel around in a circle of two hundred kilometers' circumference. When a whale is killed it is taken in tow and brought to the entrance of the bay of Cape Lopez. By a quiet little inlet on the land stands a great building with apparatus for cutting up the blubber and with great, steam-heated iron kettles in which the oil is extracted from the blubber.

When I visited these whalers I was much surprised to find that the upper jaw of the whale, from which the whale bone is cut, was thrown away into the sea as worthless. This whalebone was, until a few years ago, the most profitable part of the whale fishing.

"What's to be done about it?" the captain of the whaler said to me. "It's a question of styles. People are not wearing as many corsets as formerly, and now they are putting steel stays in them instead of whalebone."

From the oil which is tried from the blubber, various greases for lubricating leather are made in Europe. Today they also use various chemicals to take the bad taste out of the whale oil and thus make it possible to use it in manufacturing margarine.

The flesh and bones of the whale, which were once thrown away, are now ground up in big machines, boiled, treated with chemicals and made into artificial guano, which is highly valued in Europe as a fertilizer for flowers. The air in the little inlet is so poisoned by the oil and the guano that one wonders how the hundred and thirty men of the whale fisheries can, for months on end, stand this stench.

Schools of fish swarm around the whaling ships, attracted by the offal from the whales thrown into the sea. Great sharks by the dozen loiter around the landing stage.

In a four-month period about sixteen hundred whales are usually killed. One ship, fitted out with iron receptacles, stands ready to take the precious oil to Europe. Sometimes, however — no one knows why — the catch is small, and the ship goes home almost empty. This year again the outlook is not favorable. In the first fourteen days hardly a dozen whales have been caught.

[*Jagd,* pp. 9-10]

Part III

ANIMALS AND ETHICS

12

The Ethical Teaching of India

JAINISM AND AHIMSA

Jainism does not confine itself to the traditional ethics, as do the Brahmanic and Samkhya teachings, but tries also to give an ethical meaning to world- and life-negation. This endeavor explains how the commandment not to kill or harm living creatures (*Ahimsa*) first becomes important in Jainism.

The verb *hims* is the desiderative form of *han* (kill, harm). It means, therefore, the wish to kill and harm. The noun *Ahimsa* signifies, then, the renunciation of the will to kill and harm. . . .

How is the origin of the Ahimsa commandment to be explained?

It did not develop, as one might think, from a feeling of compassion. The earliest Indian thinking knew hardly anything about sympathy with the animal creation. It was, indeed, convinced of the homogeneity of all creatures through the Brahmanic idea of the universal soul. But this remained a purely theoretical conviction. Incomprehensible as it seems to us, it failed to draw the conclusion that man must sympathize with the animal creation as with his own kind.

Had it really been sympathy that gave birth to the commandment not to kill or harm, it would be impossible to understand how it could set these limits and turn away from the desire to give real help. The pretext that world- and life-negation stood in its way is not tenable. Real sympathy would have rebelled against the restrictions confining it. Nothing of the kind, however, happened.

The command not to kill or harm does not arise, then, from the feeling of compassion, but from the idea of remaining pure from the world. Originally, it belongs to the ethics of becoming perfect, not to the ethics of action. It was for his own sake, and not because of a fellow feeling for other beings, that the pious Indian of those ancient times strove with all earnestness to realize in his relations with living creatures the principle of non-activity, which springs from world- and life-negation. Violence seemed to him the action to be most avoided.

Since Jainism and the Brahmanic teaching have in common the belief in the similarity of all creatures and the principle of world- and life-negation, the Ahimsa commandment may just as well have arisen in Jainism as in Brahmanic circles. The latter is usually assumed, but the former is really more probable. Indian world- and life-negation first takes on an ethical character in Jainism. More- over the Jains from the beginning give great significance to the commandment not to kill or harm, whereas in the Upanishads it is mentioned only in passing. How is it credible, in general, that the idea of abolishing killing should have arisen among the Brahmins, who practised killing professionally in their sacrifices? Many things indicate, therefore, that the Brahmins took over the Ahimsa commandment from Jainism.

When once the Ahimsa commandment has been generally ac- cepted it has an educational influence. It arouses and keeps alive the feeling of compassion. In time it is explained, then, as arising from the motive of sympathy and is praised as behavior that comes from compassion. That it originally arose from the principle of abstaining from activity is clear from the fact that it stays within the limits of compassionate non-activity and entirely disregards helpful compassion.

In the Ayaramgasutta, a Jaina text dating probably from the third or fourth century B.C., Ahimsa is proclaimed in the following words: [1]

All saints and lords in the past, in the present, and in the future speak thus, teach thus, announce thus, and explain thus: One may not kill, mistreat, insult, torment, or persecute any form of life, any kind of creature, anything with a soul, any kind of being. This is the pure, eter- nal, enduring commandment of religion which has been proclaimed by the wise ones who understand the world.

---

[1] See Winternitz, *History of Indian Literature* (Calcutta, 1933), II, 436.

Centuries later the poet Hemacandra (twelfth century A.D.) at the wish of King Kumarapala, who had been converted to Jainism by him, discussed in a didactic poem the teaching which had become dear to the King, and praised abstention from killing and hurting in the splendid verses:

> Ahimsa is like an affectionate mother of all creatures.
> Ahimsa is like a river of nectar in the desert of Samara.
> Ahimsa is a procession of rain clouds in a forest fire of pain.
> Best herb of healing for those tormented by the disease
> Which is called the continual return of life is Ahimsa.

In obedience to the Ahimsa commandment, the Jains give up bloody sacrifices, the use of meat, hunting and animal fights. They acknowledge the obligation to be careful, as they walk, not to trample inadvertently on creeping things and insects. The Jaina monks go so far as to bind a cloth over their mouths in order not to swallow as they breathe the tiniest creatures found in the air. Jainism also feels obliged to give up work in the fields, because it is not possible to dig up the earth without injuring the smallest creatures. For this reason the Jains are mostly merchants.

The setting forth of the command not to kill or harm is one of the greatest events in the spiritual history of mankind. From its fundamental principle of refraining from activity, which is grounded in world- and life-negation, ancient Indian thought makes the tremendous discovery that ethics are boundless — and this at a time when ethics in other respects were not yet very far advanced! As far as we know this is clearly proclaimed for the first time in Jainism.

It is the great merit of Indian thought to have remained loyal to the knowledge imparted in a splendid revelation and to have recognized its significance. But it is noteworthy that it fails to study this revelation from every angle and to examine the problem inherent in it. Boundless ethics are, of course, not completely realizable. Indian thought does not come to grips with this fact. In incomprehensible fashion it clings to the illusion that not to kill or harm is completely possible for anyone who takes such commandments seriously. So the Jains pass right by the great problem as if it did not exist.

Even when a man undertakes, no matter how earnestly, to refrain from killing and hurting, he can still avoid it only to a certain extent. He is under the law of necessity which forces him to kill and to injure with or without his knowledge. It may happen in many ways that compassion is less served by slavish obedience to the command not to kill than by its violation. To put an end by a mercy killing to the suffering of a creature, when that suffering cannot be alleviated, is more ethical than to stand aloof from it. It is more cruel to let domestic animals which we can no longer feed starve painfully to death than it is to bring their lives to an end quickly and painlessly by violence. Continually we find ourselves under the necessity of saving one being by killing or injuring another.

The principle of not killing or harming should not be considered as something in itself but as the servant of compassion and subordinate to it. Therefore, it must come to terms with reality in practical fashion. A true reverence for ethics is shown in the fact that man recognizes the difficulties inherent in it.

If Indian thought were concerned with the whole of ethics and not simply with the ethics of non-activity, it could not endeavor, as it does, to avoid a practical grappling with reality.

But once again, just because it lays down the not-killing and the not-harming as dogma pure and simple, it succeeds in preserving safely through the centuries the great ethical thought bound up with it.   [*Weltanschauung*, pp. 56-61]

BUDDHISM

Buddha's Ethic of Compassion

The significance of Buddha does not lie in the realm of theoretical thought, but in this, that he spiritualizes world- and life-negation and infuses it with ethics. He makes the ethical gains of Jainism his own and carries these beginnings further.

Because Buddha proclaimed that all life is suffering, he was considered, before there was a more accurate knowledge of Jainism, to be the creator of the ethics of compassion, and men thought that the commandment not to kill or injure originated with him. This is not true. He found the Ahimsa commandment in Jainism and took it over from that source.

The Ahimsa commandment does not seem to have been so stringently observed in the older Buddhism as in Jainism. The use of meat is not strictly forbidden. Otherwise it would have been impossible to record in the holy writings of Buddhism that Buddha died after eating a dish of wild boar's flesh set before him by the smith, Cunda. It is the European scholars who are first offended by this story and try to make it appear that the word in question (*sukaramaddavam*) does not necessarily mean a dish of wild boar's meat but a dish composed of herbs, roots or mushrooms, in whose name the word "wild boar" occurred.

Now, however, we know from a saying originating with Buddha, or ascribed to him in the earliest period, that he considered the eating of flesh permissible under certain circumstances. A court doctor named Jivaka — so we are informed in Buddha's discourses — has heard that the master occasionally even eats meat and accordingly puts questions to him. Buddha thereupon explains to him that he refuses meat when he knows that the animal was slaughtered expressly for him. But he does allow himself the enjoyment of meat placed before him when he chances to arrive at mealtime, or of meat that is put in his alms-bowl. The animal, in this case, was not killed on his account; he may therefore consider this meat "irreproachable nourishment."

Paul, in the eighth chapter of the First Epistle to the Corinthians, solves in the same way the question of whether Christians may eat meat which comes from heathen sacrifices. If one is informed of its sacrificial origin, he decides, then one must not eat it, for it would be a sin. If, however, meat is served when one is invited by a heathen to a meal, or if one buys meat in the market place, then one need not inquire as to its origin and may eat it with a quiet conscience.

That Buddha should make the sophistical distinction between slaughter of which one is guilty and slaughter of which one is innocent, or that this distinction should be ascribed to him, shows that the earlier Buddhism was not yet very serious about the prohibition against meat-eating. The Buddhist monks of Ceylon still abide by this tradition. If meat is placed in their alms-bowl they eat it.

Buddha did not command his disciples to bind a cloth around

their mouths in order that they might not breathe in any living creature. Moreover, he did not object to agriculture. He did not obey the Ahimsa commandment in its details as the Jains did. He was not completely aware of the problems of the boundlessness of ethics.

Even though the commandment not to kill or injure does not originate with Buddha, he is nonetheless the creator of the ethic of compassion. For he is the one who undertakes to base on compassion the commandment which originally arose from the idea of non-activity and of keeping unsullied from the world.

In one of his discourses he describes in moving words how the vassals and mercenaries have been ordered by the king, who desires to prepare a great sacrifice, to fetch the animals chosen for the purpose, and how they begin to do it "with streaming eyes, terrified and intimidated, for fear of punishment."

He is said to have forbidden his monks the use of silk coverings, because of the representations of the silk-weavers who said that they had to be responsible for the killing of so many little creatures to get silk.

Buddha's ethic of compassion is, however, incomplete. It is limited by world- and life-negation. Nowhere does the master demand that men should strive, since all life is suffering, to bring assistance so far as possible to every human being and to every other creature. He only forbids all pitiless activity. He has no interest in compassionate service. This is excluded by the principle of non-activity, which springs from world- and life-negation.

Moreover, it is not only the principle of non-activity in Buddha that stands opposed to compassionate dealing, but also the notion of the nature of suffering, and of salvation from suffering, which goes with world- and life-negation. If all suffering arises from the will-to-live, it can be removed only by the denial of this will-to-live — that is, only by the conscious act of the being that is itself concerned. It is, indeed, purposeless to try to get relief in particular instances and from without. The basic cause of suffering remains unshaken and immediately exerts itself anew.

Compassion loses its object through world- and life-negation, which compels man — if he dares admit it to himself — to regard as purposeless and to abandon the endeavor to offer assistance to life that finds itself in distress.

As a matter of fact, Buddha's compassion consists principally in the constant realization of the fact that all creatures are continually subject to suffering. It is an intellectual sympathy rather than an immediate compassion of the heart which carries within itself the impulse to help.

We are not informed in the older tradition that Buddha spoke lovingly of animals and had an affectionate relationship with them. He was no St. Francis of Assisi.

He is first described as the great friend of animals in the Jatakas, the legendary stories of his earlier existences. One of the best known of these anecdotes tells how he delivered himself to a hungry tigress to save her from the crime of devouring her own young.

[*Weltanschauung*, pp. 100-04]

"Radiation of Kindness"

The "radiation of kindness" emanating from him [Buddha] is said to have exerted its influence not simply upon men but also upon animals. A wild elephant, which his hostile cousin Devadatta let loose upon him in a narrow lane, halted in its tracks (it is related) and, struck by the power of Buddha's kindness, let fall its trunk, which was already raised to strike.

[*Weltanschauung*, p. 80]

Lay Ethics

It is not often that Buddha expresses himself on the subject of lay ethics. Ordinarily his discourses are addressed to the monks.

From *A Discourse concerning Lay Ethics:*

But I will also tell what should be the way of life for the father of a household . . . since complete obedience to the commandments for monks is impossible for him who has a wife and a child. . . . He should kill no living thing; he should not take what is not given to him; he should not lie; he should not drink intoxicating liquors; he should refrain from lewdness. . . . Pursuant to duty he should care for his parents and follow a worthy and righteous calling.

[*Weltanschauung*, pp. 84-85]

The One-Eyed Turtle

According to Buddha it borders on the impossible that a man who has entered into a non-human form of existence because of evil-doing should later be born again as a man, "since the lower forms of being do nothing but kill each other, and know nothing of good deeds." If a yoke with a single opening is thrown into the sea — so runs a parable of Buddha — and if in the sea there is a one-eyed turtle which rises to the surface only once in a hundred years, there is a much greater probability that this turtle should some day puts its neck into the yoke with its one hole than that the fool who has once sunk to lower forms of existence should achieve again the existence of a man.

That man, in the thought of Buddha, the preacher of compassion, should be concerned only with his own salvation and not with that of all creatures, is a weakness in his teaching.

[*Weltanschauung,* pp. 87-88]

MAHAYANA BUDDHISM

In Mahayana Buddhism, Buddha's idea of compassion finds its full expression. The Mahayana believer undertakes to attain the perfection of the "great compassion." How profound is the saying "So long as living creatures suffer, there is no possibility of happiness for those who are full of compassion!" For the first time in the history of human thought, a world view is dominated by the idea of compassion.

But this mighty compassion is not able to live out its life and exert its full influence in a normal fashion. Mahayana Buddhism, like the original Buddhism, is the prisoner of world- and life-negation. Like the latter it can really call only non-activity good. Like the latter it cannot attach any real significance to the help extended for the relief of material distress. Like the latter it can recognize, as the only real deed of compassion, the spreading of the knowledge that redemption is to be had by the denial of the will-to-live.

Mahayana Buddhism is concerned for the deliverance of all creatures. How that is possible and how it may come to pass, it is no more able to explain than the Samkhya teaching and Buddha.

The hands of Mahayana compassion are bound in just the same way, then, as Buddha's hands. Fundamentally it is nothing more than the compassion of thought, which Buddha imposed upon his monks as a duty, except that all limits have been removed from it.

Therefore, it can no longer remain contemplative as it is in Buddha, but lives its life to the full in compassionate desires — often in veritable orgies of compassionate desires.

The Mahayana believer prays for all creatures, that they may suffer no want, that they may be spared pain and sickness, that they may not be abandoned or oppressed, that they may lead a happy and virtuous life, and that they may pass from the lower forms of existence into the higher forms that lead to deliverance. Long prayers of petition like this are found in the Mahayana writings. Since women are thought of as among the lower beings, the prayer for them is that they may be born again as men. Even those who dwell in the torments and anguish of hell are remembered in these prayers. The "great compassion" goes out not simply to the creatures that live on earth but to all creatures in all worlds.

From Mahayana texts: "May the fear of being devoured by each other disappear from among the animals."

[Weltanschauung, pp. 93-94]

BRAHMANISM

The Teaching of Brahmanism

All the rules dealing with caste distinctions are abrogated by need and hunger. If a member of a high caste cannot get any other kind of food, he is even permitted to eat dog's flesh offered him by a Candala.

The observance of the command not to kill or harm living creatures, except in the case of sacrifices, is strictly enjoined. Manu's Law Book even tries to take over the Jaina condemnation of agriculture. It cites as the opinion of "virtuous people" that working the soil cannot be a praiseworthy occupation, since the earth and the little living things that dwell in it are injured thereby. At the same time it concedes, however, that others may even consider it to be a good thing.

The Brahmin must expiate for the annihilation of thousands of little vertebrates in the same way as he must for the killing of a member of the lowest caste. If he has cut down fruit trees, bushes, climbing plants or flowers, he must repeat a hundred times a certain text from the Vedas.

In general the recitation of the Veda, and sacrifice and asceticism, wipe out guilt. Some value is placed even upon the confession of a transgression: "If a man who has committed a sin confesses it voluntarily, he is freed from it, just as a snake sloughs off its skin."

Asceticism has the highest expiatory value. When it is strictly practised, the greatest crimes may be atoned for. "Even insects, snakes, butterflies, birds and plants reach heaven by virtue of asceticism." The problem of world redemption is not foreign to Manu's Law Book. [*Weltanschauung,* pp. 134-35]

Sacrificial Slaying

The Brahmin must observe strictly the rule not to kill or harm (Ahimsa). But sacrificial slaying is permitted, and the Brahmin is allowed to eat the meat of the sacrifice.

[*Weltanschauung,* p. 167]

HINDUISM

Hindu Ethics

Hinduism is much more strongly concerned with ethics than the Brahmanic teaching:

He who hates no living creature, who is affectionate and compassionate, who is without egotism and selfishness, who considers pain and pleasure equal, who is patient, contented, always humble, completely self-controlled and strongly determined, he who fixes his mind and reason on me and loves me, he is dear to me.

[*Weltanschauung,* p. 151]

GANDHI

Gandhi's feeling for reality is seen in his relations to the Ahimsa commandment. He is not satisfied with praising it, but examines it critically. He is concerned at the fact that in spite of the authority of this commandment there is in India such a lack of pity both for animals and for mankind. He ventures to say: "I hardly think the fate of animals is so sad in any other country in the world as it is in our own poor India. We cannot make the English responsible for this; nor can we excuse ourselves by pleading our poverty. Criminal neglect is the only cause of the deplorable condition of our cattle."

The fact that the Ahimsa commandment has not educated the people to a really compassionate attitude he attributes to its having been followed more in the letter than in the spirit. People have thought they were obeying it sufficiently by avoiding killing and the causing of pain — whereas in reality the commandment is only fulfilled by the complete practice of compassion.

It is not clear to Gandhi that it belongs to the original nature of the Ahimsa commandment to demand only abstinence from killing and hurting and not the complete exercise of compassion. He took it upon himself to go beyond the letter of the law against killing, and this, moreover, in a case where he came into conflict with the Hindu reverence for horned cattle. He ended the sufferings of a calf in its prolonged death agony by giving it poison. By this act he caused his Hindu adherents no less offense than when for the first time he received untouchables at his settlement (Ashram).

Thus in Gandhi's ethical life-affirmation, Ahimsa is freed from the principle of non-activity in which it originated and becomes a commandment to exercise full compassion. It becomes a different thing from what it was in the thought of ancient India.

And through his feeling for reality, Gandhi also arrives at the admission that the commandment not to kill or injure cannot be carried out in entirety, because man cannot maintain life without committing acts of violence. So with a heavy heart he gives permission to kill dangerous snakes and allows the farmer to defend himself against the monkeys which threaten his harvest.

It is one of the most important of Gandhi's acts that he compels Indian ethics to come to grips with reality. [*Indian*, pp. 229-30] [1]

---

[1] This passage does not occur in the German edition published in Munich in 1935 by C. H. Beck'sche Verlagsbuchhandlung. [*Editor's note.*]

13

The Ethical Teaching of China and Tibet

TIBETAN BUDDHISM

The command not to kill living creatures is observed by the Buddhists of Tibet only in a very superficial way. They think they are obeying the rule when they abstain from bloody sacrifice. When, therefore, they crave meat from one of the herd animals, they suffocate it painfully by holding its mouth and nose.

[*Weltanschauung*, p. 112]

THE KAN-YING-P'IEN

Chinese ethics also reach the point of concern for the problem of man and the animal creation. Here, however, the kindly treatment of all creatures is based upon the relationship existing between them and mankind and upon natural sympathy. Moreover, it is not limited to not-killing and not-injuring; active compassion is commanded.

The *Kan-Ying P'ien* (*The Book of Rewards and Punishments*) goes furthest in its demand for sympathy with animals. This book is a popular writing originating at about the time of the Sung Dynasty (960-1227 A.D.) — that is to say, in the renaissance of Chinese thought — and is today still among the most widely read books of Chinese literature. It contains a collection of two hundred and twelve sentences, mostly very short, about good and evil, the sentences being probably much older than the book itself.

There are editions of this book in which every saying is accompanied by a short explanation and elucidated by several anecdotes.

Commandments of the *Kan-Ying-P'ien:*

156

Have a merciful heart for all creatures.

One should not hurt even worms and insects and plants and trees.

He does wrong . . . who shoots birds, hunts animals, digs up the larvae of insects, frightens nesting birds, stops up burrows, carries off nests, wounds pregnant animals . . . does not permit man and beast to rest.

From the explanations of the commandments:

If a man sees animals in need, he must take heed to help them and to preserve their lives.

Do not let your children amuse themselves by making toys out of flies, or butterflies or little birds. It is not simply that such behavior results in injury to living creatures, but also because it arouses in young hearts an impulse to cruelty and murder.

Heaven and earth give life and growth to all beings. Whenever you injure them, you do not comply with the kindness of heaven and earth.

Stories illustrative of the commandments:

The wife of a soldier named Fan was tuberculous and close to death. She was ordered to eat the brains of a hundred sparrows as a remedy. When she saw the birds in the cage, she sighed and said: "Must it be that a hundred living creatures are to be killed that I may be healed? I would rather die than permit them to suffer." She opened the cage and allowed them to fly away. A little while afterwards she recovered from her illness.

Tsao-Pin lived in a ruined house. His children begged him to have it repaired. But he answered them saying: "In the cold of winter the cracks in the walls and the space between the tiles and between the stones provide a shelter and a refuge to all kinds of living creatures. We should not endanger their lives."

Wu-Tang, from Liu-Ling, used to take his son hunting with him. One day they came upon a stag that was playing with its young one. When it caught sight of Tang it fled. Tang, however, took an arrow and killed the young one. The frightened stag ran off with a cry of anguish. When Tang had concealed himself in the tall grass the stag returned and licked the wounds of its fawn. Once more Tang drew his bow and killed it. Shortly after he saw another stag and sent an arrow flying towards it. But the arrow was deflected and pierced his son. Thereupon Tang threw his bow away and tearfully embraced his son. At the same moment he heard a voice from the air that said to him: "Tang, the stag loved its fawn as much as you loved your son."

The ethics of love for all living creatures advocated by the *Kan-Ying-P'ien* has been explained by the influence upon Chinese ethics of the Indian Ahimsa commandment. This has nothing to do with it. Buddhism, of course, was widespread in China during the early centuries of the Christian era, and even in the form of Mahayana Buddhism, which inculcates the duty of mercifulness to all creatures much more insistently than Buddha himself. But nowhere in the *Kan-Ying-P'ien* is evident the special character of Indian compassion, which is based entirely upon a world view of world- and life-negation. Chinese thought passes independently from the idea of love for men, as it is found in Confucius (Kung-tse, 551-479 B.C.), Mi-tse (died about 400 B.C.), and Meng-tse (372-289 B.C.), to that of love for all creatures. This development was surely furthered through acquaintance with Buddhism and the Indian Ahimsa commandment. But even in Meng-tse, long before Buddhism came to China, a far-reaching compassion for animals is evident. Meng-tse praises King Süan of Tsi because of his compassion in freeing an ox that was to be sacrificed at the dedication of some bells. Such a sentiment, he says, should suffice to make one king of the world.

Individual sayings of the *Kan-Ying-P'ien* reveal acquaintance with the Indian Ahimsa commandment. But the spirit of its ethic of boundless sympathy is not Indian.

[*Weltanschauung,* pp. 61-63]

MONASTIC TAOISM

From the commandments for monks in the present-day monastic Taoism of China:

1st commandment:	Thou shalt kill no living thing nor do injury to its life.
2nd commandment:	Thou shalt not consume as food the flesh and blood of any living creature.

The well-known commandments for compassion toward all creatures from the *Kan-Ying-P'ien* are also found in these rules for monks:

34th commandment:	Thou shalt not . . . strike or whip domestic animals.
35th commandment:	Thou shalt not intentionally crush insects and ants with thy foot.

36th commandment: Thou shalt not play with hooks and arrows for thine own amusement.

37th commandment: Thou shalt not climb into trees to remove nests and to destroy the eggs.

63d commandment: Thou shalt not catch birds and quadrupeds with snares and nets.

64th commandment: Thou shalt not frighten and scare away birds that are brooding on their nests.

65th commandment: Thou shalt not pluck or pull up flowers and grass without a reason.

66th commandment: Thou shalt not cut down trees without a reason.

67th commandment: Thou shalt not burn pastures or mountain forests.

68th commandment: Thou shalt not dig up during the winter months animals hibernating in the earth.

112th commandment: Thou shalt not pour hot water on the ground in order to exterminate insects and ants.

[*Weltanschauung*, pp. 106-07]

14

The Necessity for a Complete Ethic in the West

How far Kant is removed from comprehending the problem of a basic ethical principle which has a definite content is evident from the fact that he clings persistently to a very narrow conception of the domain of ethics. He permits ethics to concern itself only with the duties of man to man. He does not include in it man's relation to the non-human creature. Only indirectly does he bring within the field of ethics the prohibition of animal torture; he includes this under the duties of man toward himself. Sympathy with the suffering of animals, he says, is dulled in us by our cruel treatment of them, and thereby "a natural disposition which is very useful to morality in respect to other men is weakened and gradually eradicated."

Moreover, the vandalism involved in the destruction of the beautiful creations of nature, which are thought to be without feeling, is only to be considered unethical in so far as it contradicts man's duty to himself, by doing violence to the desire to have something to love of no utilitarian value — a desire which in itself strengthens morality.

If the domain of ethics is limited to the relations of man to man, then every effort to arrive at a fundamental ethical principle which has an absolutely binding content is hopeless from the beginning. The absolute and the universal belong together. If there really is a fundamental principle of ethics, it must somehow refer to the relation of man to life as such in all of its manifestations.

Kant, therefore, does not approach the task of developing an

162

ethic which corresponds to his deepened conception of the ethical. On the whole he does nothing more than take the utilitarian ethic which he found under the protection of the categorical imperative. Behind an imposing facade he erects a tenement house.

[*Kultur,* pp. 105-06]

SCHOPENHAUER

Ethics is compassion. All life is suffering. The conscious will-to-live is filled, therefore, with the deepest pity for all creatures; it is particularly aware not only of the woes of mankind but also of those of the creatures that suffer with it. In ethics, what we usually call "love" is, in its true character, pity. In this great compassion, the will-to-live is turned away from itself, and its purification begins.

How concerned are Kant, Hegel and others to deprive direct compassion of its rightful place in ethics, because it does not conform to their theories! But Schopenhauer pulls the gag from its mouth and bids it speak. Those who, like Fichte, Schleiermacher and others, base the ethical upon a world-purpose which they have laboriously thought out expect a man to run continually up to the topmost storeroom of his reflections in order to fetch down the motives for moral behavior. In accordance with the utilitarians of the social sciences, he is always supposed to sit down first and figure out what is ethical. Schopenhauer tells him to heed his own heart — something unheard of in philosophical ethics. Elementary ethics, which has been shoved into a corner by the others, comes into its own again through him.

The others, in order not to get into difficulties with their theories, must confine ethics exclusively to man's relation to man. They anxiously teach that pity for animals is not ethical in itself, but gets its meaning only by reference to the kindly disposition which must be preserved among men. Schopenhauer demolishes these fences and teaches love for the most miserable creature.

[*Kultur,* p. 165]

THE WILL-TO-LIVE

Men's will-to-live is frequently translated into something like an intoxication. The sunshine of spring, trees in blossom, fleeting clouds, waving fields, all stimulate it. The will-to-live revealed around them in manifold splendid forms carries their own will-to-live along with it. With exultant desire they would join in the great symphony they hear. The world seems beautiful to them. . . . But the intoxication passes off. Where they thought they heard music they once more hear only the noise of dreadful discords. The beauty of nature is darkened by the suffering they find everywhere in it. They perceive again that they are being driven like shipwrecked men on a watery waste, their boat now lifted up upon mountainous waves and now plunged into the trough of the sea, the billows sometimes bright in the sun's rays and now dark under heavy clouds.

Now they would like to convince themselves that there is land in the direction in which they are driven. Their will-to-live deludes them so that they endeavor to see the world as they would like to see it. They force their thought to provide them with a chart that confirms their hope for land. Once again they bend to the oars, until once again their arms sink wearily and their disappointed eyes wander from billow to billow.

This is the voyage of the will-to-live which has abandoned thought.

Does there remain, then, nothing for the will-to-live except to be driven along without thought or to sink in pessimistic knowledge? No. It must travel the boundless sea. But it may set sail and steer a certain course.

The will-to-live that wants to know the world is a shipwrecked man; the will-to-live that comes to know itself is a bold mariner.

[*Kultur,* pp. 208-09]

THE IRON DOOR GIVES WAY

For long months I lived in a constant state of inner excitement. Without any success I concentrated my thinking upon the nature of world- and life-affirmation and of ethics, and on what they had in common, with no let-up even during the daily work of the hospital. I was wandering about in a thicket, in which no path was to be found. I was leaning against an iron door, which would not give before me. . . .

In this state I had to undertake a rather long journey on the river. While my wife and I were staying because of her health at

Cape Lopez by the sea — it was in September 1915 — I was called to visit Mrs. Pelot, the sick wife of a missionary, at N'Gomo, about two hundred kilometers upstream. The only means of conveyance I could find was a little steamer towing an overladen barge, already on the point of departure. Except for myself there were only blacks on board, among them Emil Ogouma, my friend from Lambarene. As I had not been able in my hurry to provide sufficient food, they permitted me to eat with them out of their cooking pot.

Slowly we crept upstream, carefully picking our way among the sandbanks — it was the dry season. Lost in thought, I sat on the deck of the barge, struggling to find the elementary and universal notion of ethics, which I had not discovered in any philosophy. Sheet after sheet of paper I covered with unconnected sentences, just in order to keep my mind concentrated on the problem. At sunset on the evening of the third day, as we were passing through a herd of hippopotamuses, there came to me suddenly, unpresaged and unsought, the words "Reverence for Life." The iron door had given way; the path in the thicket had become plain. I had now forced my way to the idea in which world- and life-affirmation and ethics were both contained! Now I knew that ethical world- and life-affirmation, along with its ideals of civilization, was founded on thought.   [*Leben,* pp. 135-36]

THE UNIVERSALIZING OF SELF-DEVOTION

If the ethics of self-devotion is to be reconciled with the ethics of self-realization, it must likewise become universal, and self-devotion must be directed not only towards man and society but also towards the life which is everywhere manifest in the world.

But ethics up to this point has been unwilling to take even the first step towards this universalizing of self-devotion.

Just as the housewife who has scrubbed the room takes good care that the door is shut so that the dog may not enter and, with the prints of its paws, undo the work she has done, so European thinkers see to it that no animals run around in their ethics. The follies they commit in order to maintain the traditional narrow-mindedness and to make a principle out of it border on the unbelievable. Either they let all sympathy for animals escape or they see to it that it shrinks to a meaningless residue. If they permit anything more to emerge, then they think themselves obliged to produce far-fetched justifications for it, if not excuses.

It is as if Descartes had bewitched the whole of European philosophy with his declaration that animals were nothing but machines.

As important a thinker as Wilhelm Wundt disfigures his ethics with the following sentences:

The only object of sympathy is man. The animals are our "fellow-creatures," an expression by which language already hints at the fact that we acknowledge here a kind of relationship only with reference to the ultimate basis of being, creation. Emotions which to a certain degree resemble sympathy may, therefore, arise even in relation to the animals, but for genuine sympathy, the basic condition of inner sympathy of our will with theirs is lacking.

To crown this wisdom he makes the final assertion that in any case there can be no question of rejoicing with the animals — as though he had never seen a thirsty ox drink.

Kant expressly emphasizes the fact that ethics deals only with the duties of man to man. He thinks he must justify the "human" treatment of animals by setting it up as the practice of a sensibility which improves our sympathetic relations with men.

Bentham, too, defends mercy for animals principally as a means of preventing the emergence of a heartless attitude towards men, even though he admits occasionally that it is inherently right.

Darwin in his *Descent of Man* mentions the fact that the feeling of sympathy which dominates the social instinct becomes in the end so strong that it includes all mankind, and even animals. But he does not pursue the problem any further, and contents himself with setting forth the ethics of the human herd.

In European thought, therefore, it amounts to a dogma that ethics deals only with the relations of man to man and to society. The suggestions that come from Schopenhauer, Stern and a few others — to the effect that the antiquated ramparts should be razed — are not understood.

This backwardness is all the more incomprehensible in that Indian and Chinese thought, almost before it had begun to develop, based ethics on kindly relations with all creatures. Moreover, these two systems of thought came to this conviction quite independently of each other. The commandments concerning consideration for animals which are so beautiful and so far-reaching, in the popular Chinese ethics of the *Kan-Ying-P'ien* (*The Book of Rewards and Punishments*)[1] do not, as is commonly assumed, stem from Buddhist influences. They have no connection with the metaphysical discussions about the interdependence of all beings which were current in Indian thought as the ethical horizon widened; but they come out of a vital, ethical feeling which dares to draw the consequences that seem natural to it.

When European thought resists the universalizing of self-devotion, the reason is that it is striving for a rational ethic that offers universally valid judgments. There is no prospect of reaching such an ethic except when man keeps his feet on firm ground and considers only the interests of human society. An ethic which is occupied with the relations between men and the animal creation, however, leaves that ground, and is driven into the discussion of existence as such. Willingly or unwillingly, ethics must plunge into the adventure of making its adjustment with nature philosophy, the outcome of which cannot be anticipated.

This is true. But it has already been shown that the objective, standard ethics of society, if it can really be set forth in this way, is never true ethics, but only an appendix to it. It is further clear that genuine ethics is always subjective, that irrational enthusiasm is the very breath of its life, and that it must be distinguished from nature philosophy. The ethic of self-devotion has no reason at all, therefore, for holding itself aloof from an adventure which is in any case unavoidable. Its house has burned down. Let it go forth into the world to seek its fortune.

Let it dare, then, to accept the thought that self-devotion must stretch out not simply to mankind but to all creation, and especially

[1] This book dates from about the eleventh century A.D. It has been translated into English by James Legge (*Sacred Books of the East*, 1891), and by T. Susuki and P. Carus (Chicago, 1906); and into French by M. A. Rémusat (*Le Livre des récompenses et des peines*, 1816), and by Stanislas Julien (1835); into German by W. Schüler (*Zeitschrift für Missionskunde*, 1909).

"Be humane to animals, do no harm even to insects, plants and trees," one saying of this book enjoins. The following acts are wrong: "Running down men and animals, shooting birds with arrows; hunting quadrupeds; driving insects out of their holes; frightening birds asleep in the trees; stopping up the holes of insects and destroying the nests of birds." Delight in hunting is described as a serious moral perversion.

to all life in the world within the reach of man. Let it rise to the conception that the relation of man to man is only an expression of the relation in which he stands to all being and to the world in general. The ethic of self-devotion, having thus become cosmic, can hope to meet the ethic of self-realization, which is cosmic by nature, and to unite with it.   [*Kultur,* pp. 225-28]

IT IS GOOD TO MAINTAIN LIFE

Descartes' philosophizing begins with the sentence, "I think, therefore I am." With this miserable, arbitrarily chosen beginning, it finds itself irrevocably committed on the road to the abstract. It never finds the door to ethics and it is caught like a prisoner in a dead world- and life-view.

True philosophy must proceed from the most immediate and comprehensive fact of consciousness — "I am life that wills to live in the midst of life that wills to live." This is not a subtly reasoned dogma. Day by day, hour by hour, I move in it. In every moment of reflection it stands before me anew. A vital world- and life-view that sees into all the facts of being bursts continuously forth from it as from never-withering roots. The mysticism of ethical communion with being grows out of it.

As in my own will-to-live I feel a longing for a richer life and for that mysterious exaltation of the will-to-live which we call pleasure, and as I dread annihilation and that mysterious depreciation of the will-to-live which we call pain, the same is true of the will-to-live around me, whether it can express itself or remains dumb before me.

Ethics, therefore, consists in this: I feel a compulsion to extend to all the will-to-live around me the same reverence for life that I extend to my own. The fundamental principle of morality so necessary for thought is given here. It is good to maintain life and to promote life; it is evil to destroy life and to restrict life.

In truth, everything that is considered good in the usual ethical appraisal of the behavior of men toward one another can be reduced to the material and spiritual maintenance or promotion of human life, and the effort to bring it to its highest worth. On the contrary, everything that is considered evil in the behavior of men to one another is, in the last analysis, the material or spiritual destruction or obstruction of human life, or negligence in striving to bring it to its highest value. Separate categories of good and evil, lying far apart and apparently completely unrelated, fit together in coherent pieces, as soon as their profound significance is comprehended under this most universal definition of good and evil.

This basic principle of ethics so necessary for thought means, however, not simply the ordering and deepening of the accepted notions of good and evil, but also their broadening. Only that man is truly ethical who feels the necessity of assisting all life that he is able to help, and who shrinks from inflicting harm upon any living creature. He does not inquire to what degree this or that life merits our sympathy as worthy, nor whether and to what degree it is as yet capable of feeling. Life as such is sacred to him. He breaks no leaf from the tree, he plucks no flower, he is careful to crush no insect with his feet. When he works by his lamp in the summer evening, he prefers to keep his window shut and to breathe the stifling air rather than to see insect after insect falling on his table with singed wings.

If after a rain he is walking on the road and sees an earthworm which has gone astray, he remembers that it will dry up in the sun if it does not get back in time to the earth into which it can burrow, and helps it from the fatal stones into the grass. If he comes upon an insect that has fallen into a puddle, he takes time to save it by extending a leaf or a stalk to it.

He is not afraid of being laughed at as sentimental. It is the fate of every truth to be ridiculed before it is recognized. It was once considered stupid to think that colored men were really human and must be treated humanely. This stupidity has become a truth. Today it is thought an exaggeration to state that a reasonable ethic demands constant consideration for all living things down to the lowliest manifestations of life. The time is coming, however, when people will be amazed that it took so long for mankind to recognize that thoughtless injury to life was incompatible with ethics.

Ethics is responsibility for all that lives — extended until it knows no limits.

The definition of ethics as behavior based on the conviction of reverence for life leaves one, in general, unmoved. But it is the only complete definition. Sympathy is too narrow a thing to be ranked as the sum total of the ethical. It denotes, indeed, only compassion for the suffering will-to-live. Part of ethics is that we should experience in ourselves all the circumstances and all the aspirations of the will-to-live, its joy, its longing to live out its life, as well as its urge to self-realization.

Love already means more, since it comprehends within itself a fellowship in pain and joy and striving. But it reveals the ethical only in an allegory, even though this is a natural and profound parable. It makes the solidarity produced by ethics analogous to that which nature introduces on the physical plane in a more or less temporary fashion between two beings who complete themselves sexually — or between parents and their children.

We must strive in our thinking to bring out the inner nature of the ethical. We come in this way to define ethics as devotion to life which is inspired by reverence for life. Though the phrase *reverence for life* may sound so general as to be rather lifeless, nonetheless its meaning is something that never leaves a man into whose thought it has once penetrated. Sympathy and love and in general every precious enthusiasm are contained within it. With an unresting, vital force, reverence for life works upon the mind it has entered and throws it into the disquietude of a responsibility which never ceases. Reverence for life drives a man on as a churning screw drives a ship through the water.

The ethic of reverence for life, arising as it does from inner necessity, is not dependent upon the extent, great or little, to which it can be thought out as a satisfying conception of life. It does not have to give an answer as to the significance for the total course of world events of the striving of an ethical man to maintain, promote and enhance life. It does not permit itself to be confused by the thought that the maintenance and fulfillment of life which it has practised is hardly worth notice in comparison with the tremendous and ceaseless destruction of life which constantly takes place through natural forces. With its will to work, it can leave aside all the problems concerning the result of its work. It is significant for the world that there has appeared in it, through the ethically sensitive man, a will-to-live filled with reverence for life and devotion to life.

In my will-to-live the universal will-to-live reveals itself in a fashion different from its other manifestations. In these others it appears in an individualization which, so far as I can see from without, is bent only upon living its own life and not at all upon identifying itself with any other will-to-live. The world is a cruel drama of the will-to-live divided against itself. One existence prevails at the expense of another; one destroys another. One will-to-live merely exerts its will against another, without being conscious of other wills-to-live. A longing to attain unity with itself and to become universal is not found in it.

Why does the will-to-live have this experience only in me? Is it because I have acquired the ability to reflect upon the totality of existence? Where is this evolution begun in me leading?

There is no answer to these questions. It remains a painful enigma for me that I must live with reverence for life in a world ruled by a creative will which is at the same time a destructive will, and by a destructive will which is at the same time a creative will.

I cannot do otherwise than cling to the fact that in me the will-to-live strives to be one with other wills-to-live. That is the light that shines in my darkness. The ignorance with which the world is filled is taken away from me. I have been saved from the world. I am thrown by reverence for life into an unrest which the world does not know. I receive from it a blessedness which the world cannot give. When another person and I help each other with understanding and forgiveness because of the tenderness produced by our difference from the world — where otherwise one will would torment another — the division of the will-to-live within itself is removed. When I rescue an insect from the puddle, then life has given itself to life, and the division of life within itself has ceased. When my life devotes itself to another life in any way whatever, my finite will-to-live communes with the infinite will in which all life is one. I find refreshment which keeps me from dying of thirst in the desert of life.   [*Kultur*, pp. 242-46]

CREATURES AID ONE ANOTHER

Wherever we find the love and sacrificial care of parents for offspring we find ethical power. Indeed any instance of creatures giving aid to one another reveals it. Moreover, there are probably more proofs than we might think. Let me tell you of three instances which have been brought to my attention.

The first example was told me by someone in Scotland. It happened in a park where a flock of wild geese had settled to rest on a pond. One of the flock had been captured by a gardener, who had clipped its wings before releasing it. When the geese started to resume their flight, this one tried frantically, but vainly, to lift itself into the air. The others, observing his struggles, flew about in obvious efforts to encourage him; but it was no use. Thereupon the entire flock settled back on the pond and waited, even though the urge to go on was strong within them. For several days they waited until the damaged feathers had grown sufficiently to permit the goose to fly. Meanwhile the unethical gardener, having been converted by the ethical geese, gladly watched them as they finally rose together, and resumed their long flight.

My second example is from my hospital in Lambarene. I have the virtue of caring for all stray monkeys that come to our gate. (If you have had any experience with large numbers of monkeys, you know why I say it is a "virtue" thus to take care of all comers until they are old enough or strong enough to be turned loose, several together, in the forest — a great occasion for them and for me!) Sometimes there will come to our monkey colony a wee baby monkey whose mother has been killed, leaving this orphaned infant. I have to find one of the older monkeys to adopt and care for the baby. I never have any difficulty about it, except to decide which candidate shall be given the responsibility. Many a time it happens that the seemingly worst-tempered monkeys are most insistent upon having this sudden burden of foster parenthood given to them.

My third example was given me by a friend in Hanover, who owned a small café. He would daily throw out crumbs for the sparrows in the neighborhood. He noticed that one sparrow was injured, so that it had difficulty getting about. But he was interested to discover that the other sparrows, apparently by mutual agreement, would leave the crumbs which lay nearest their crippled comrade, so that he could get his share, undisturbed.

[*Reverence*, pp. 238-39]

SYMPATHY IN SAVAGE BREASTS

That sympathy toward unfortunate creatures can be awakened in even the most savage of beings I learn while the piles are being set. Before the pile is placed in the hole I always look to see if any ants, toads, or other creatures have fallen into it, and if so I take them out with my hands, that they may not be crushed by the pile or later killed by the pounding down of earth and stones. I explain my action to those who are working with me. Some of them are puzzled and smile, others let the words they have heard so often pass over them indifferently.

One day a real savage who was setting out piles with me was detailed to Mrs. Russell, with others, to cut down underbrush. A toad was spied in the midst of it, and his neighbor started to kill it with his bushknife. The first man seized his arm, however, and developed for him and the listening crew of men the theory that the animals had also been created by the dear God, and that he would hold a big palaver with the men who tortured or killed them. This savage was the last upon whom I should have supposed that my actions and words while setting the piles would have made any impression.   [*Mitteilungen*, III, p. 40]

WHAT LIFE MUST WE SACRIFICE?

All life is holy to the truly ethical man — even that which from the human standpoint seems to be lower life. This man makes distinctions under the force of necessity, as cases arise when he must decide what life he must sacrifice for the sake of another life. As he makes this decision in case after case, he is aware that his procedure is subjective and arbitrary, and that he must bear the responsibility for the life that is sacrificed.

I rejoice over the new methods of treating sleeping sickness, which permit me to save life where previously I could only watch a painful infirmity. Every time that I place under the microscope the agent of sleeping sickness, however, I cannot but think that I have to annihilate this life in order to save another.

From the natives I buy a young fish eagle, which they have caught on a sandbank, in order to rescue it from their cruel hands. But now I must decide whether I shall let it starve, or whether I shall kill a certain number of small fish every day in order to keep it alive. I decide upon the latter course. But every day I find it rather hard to sacrifice — upon my own responsibility — one life for another.

Standing as he does with every other creature, under the law of the will-to-live, with its inner inconsistency, the human being finds himself again and again in the position of being able to preserve his own life and life in general only at the cost of other life. If he is moved by the ethics of reverence for life, he injures and destroys life only under the compulsion of a necessity which he cannot escape, never from thoughtlessness. If he is a free man, he seeks, so far as he has the opportunity, to taste the blessedness of being able to sustain life and of protecting it from pain and annihilation.

Since from youth on I have been devoted to the cause of animal protection, it gives me a peculiar delight to find that the universal ethics of reverence for life proves that sympathy for animals, which is so often represented as sentimentality, is something which no thinking individual can avoid. Earlier ethical systems faced the problem of man and beast either uncomprehendingly or helplessly. Even when it was felt that sympathy for animals was right, this sympathy could not be co-ordinated with ethics, since ethics was really concerned only with the behavior of man to man.

When will public opinion no longer sanction popular entertainment which consists in the mistreatment of animals?

[*Leben,* pp. 202-03]

FALCONRY ONCE MORE

In the *Atlantis,* which I read regularly and with great interest here in the jungle, I find a report of efforts now being made to bring back into popularity the sport of falconry which was long ago abandoned. It ends with this sentence: "This beautiful old hunting game, once the delight of princes *par excellence,* is beginning to be a romantic sport."

As a friend of nature, I must state that I should greatly regret the revival of this cruel form of hunting unfortunate birds; and I cherish the hope that it will not again be successfully introduced. Is there a friend of nature who really finds pleasure in the tragic spectacle of the abuse and killing of a weak bird by a strong one,

and who, by training birds of prey, takes pains to see that this spectacle shall be offered him as frequently as possible? And what is there "romantic" in this "sport"? Is it that the men of an earlier — and in many respects a thoughtless and inhumane — age indulged in it?

This form of hunting was given up when the men of the Age of Enlightenment perceived the horror, not only of torture, but also of many another kind of cruelty, which had not been sufficiently understood up to that time. Today, on the contrary, we are slowly coming again to the point where customs we thought had been abandoned forever as incompatible with true manhood seem likely to be adopted once more.

The natural human feeling that revolts against the revival of something that should be definitely relegated to the past is said to be a sentimentality with which we must dispense — because it stands in the way of the education of the race in vigor.

Falconry, moreover, is commended because it appears in the guise of sport and love of nature. It has no just claim to be associated with either. Sport is physical exercise — not watching a weak creature tortured by a strong one until it falls prey to it. The friend of nature is the man who feels himself inwardly united with everything that lives in nature, who shares in the fate of all creatures, helps them when he can in their pain and need, and as far as possible avoids injuring or taking life.

We must never permit the voice of humanity within us to be silenced. It is man's sympathy with all creatures that first makes him truly a man.

And now are we to stand still or go backwards — rather than go forward in true manhood?

First among the explanations we hear from the lovers of cruel practices is the statement that nature herself is full of cruelty. True — but this does not remove my guilt when, because of my thoughtlessness or my delight in the drama of battle, I still further increase the existing measure of woe and suffering.

The fact that in nature one creature may cause pain to another and even deal with it instinctively in the most cruel way, is a harsh mystery that weighs upon us as long as we live. One who has reached the point where he does not suffer ever and again because of this has really ceased to be a man. We, too, are under the law of necessity when — to prolong our own existence — we must bring other creatures to a painful end. But we should never cease to consider this as something tragic and incomprehensible. Only so far as a compelling necessity exists for it can we accept responsibility for the pain and destruction that we ourselves cause living things. Where we have a choice, we must avoid bringing torment and injury into the life of another, even the lowliest of creatures; to do so is to shoulder a guilt which nothing justifies and renounce our manhood.

The struggle for existence that takes place all around us among living creatures can never be — unless we have succumbed to thoughtlessness — a spectacle to watch with interest and delight, but always a painful one. Torture and killing can never become a noble and satisfying sport to us: let no one disturb us with talk about "noble sport." Animals destructive to crops or otherwise harmful must be shot. Only that hunting is noble, however, which is carried on with the intention of killing the animals as quickly and as painlessly as possible. When, on the contrary, the animal is expected both to provide an exciting spectacle of pursuit and to suffer a thousand death agonies before it has fulfilled its destiny, or when, as in falconry, herons and other birds, for whose slaughter there is no excuse, are hunted simply for the sake of the interesting sight of their vain efforts to escape, then it cannot be a question of "noble sport," and it is to be hoped that this term may, indeed, be abandoned.

It is a disgrace to our time that animal fights are still being staged everywhere, including bull fights, cock fights and many other cruel diversions in southern countries. In certain southern regions the Sunday pastime consists in giving a rat to a dog in a wire cage; young and old watch with excitement the vain fight which the rat puts up for its life. And now when we should bend all our efforts to get rid of the last remnants of such customs, which brutalize every feeling of humanity, voices are again raised in favor of the cruel hunting with falcons as a romantic sport for nature lovers.

Is it really a proper task for the ornithological station at Rossitten, which was founded by the state in 1901 for the study of bird migration, and which counts so many friends among animal lovers, to concern itself with the training of birds of prey, and with making popular again this cruel form of hunting?

When the free bird of prey kills weaker birds in order to get food for itself and its brood, it is acting in accordance with natural instincts. We have even learned that the species of bird pursued is thereby kept healthy, since the birds weakened by sickness — a source of infection for their own kind — most easily fall victim.

We can do nothing about the cruelty which exists among nature's living creatures. We ourselves, however, as people who have learned wisdom, must not train animals to provide entertainment for us by the cruel murder of their poor victims. Our own vocation is not to acquiesce in the cruelty of nature and even join in it, but rather to set a limit to it so far as our influence reaches. With deep reverence for life and with profound sympathy for suffering and anguish, it is up to us to show mercy and to offer deliverance to those who crave it. Since we are so often compelled by necessity to bring pain and death to living creatures, it is all the more incumbent upon us, when we *can* act as free beings, to help rather than harm these creatures.

The thinking man must therefore oppose all cruel customs no matter how deeply rooted in tradition and surrounded by a halo. True manhood is too precious a spiritual good for us to surrender any part of it to thoughtlessness.

Very little of the great cruelty shown by men can really be attributed to cruel instinct. Most of it comes from thoughtlessness or inherited habit. The roots of cruelty, therefore, are not so much strong as widespread. But the time must come when inhumanity protected by custom and thoughtlessness will succumb before humanity championed by thought.

Let us work that this time may come.   [*Falkenjägerei*]

PART IV

REVERENCE FOR LIFE

15

Philosophy and the Movement
for the Protection of Animals

The movement for the protection of animals has received no support from European philosophy. Philosophy has either regarded the expression of practical sympathy with the animal creation as a piece of sentimentality which has nothing to do with reasonable ethics or has attributed to it a rather secondary importance. For Descartes, animals were only machines and did not need our sympathy. The English ethical thinker Jeremy Bentham (1748-1832) regarded kindness to animals chiefly as practice for kindness to men. Kant's judgment was the same. He expressly emphasized the opinion that ethics are really concerned only with the duties of man to man.

European philosophy tries to hold fast to this fundamental principle even when it is sympathetic to the movement for the protection of animals. It cannot make up its mind to take the decisive step of making kindness to animals an ethical demand, on exactly the same footing as kindness to human beings.

In Chinese and Indian thought the responsibility of man to the animal creation plays a much greater part than in European thought.

The Chinese philosopher Meng-tse (372-289 B.C.), who belonged to the school of Confucius (552-479 B.C.), speaks most impressively of sympathy with animals. Lieh-tse, of the school of Lao-tse (sixth century B.C.), expresses his conviction that the hearts and minds of animals are not so different from those of men as is generally assumed. Yang-Dehu disputes the prejudiced belief that other creatures exist only for the sake and for the use of human beings. Their existence, he says, has an independent significance and value.

Sympathy with animals plays a great part in the *Kan-Ying-P'ien* (*The Book of Rewards and Punishments*), a Chinese collection of one hundred and twelve ethical maxims, dating from the time of the Sung Dynasty (960-1227 A.D.). The maxims themselves are probably much older. In this collection of maxims, which even today is highly esteemed among the Chinese, we find expressed the thought that "Heaven" (that is, God) gives life to all creatures. So in order to be in harmony with "Heaven" we must behave kindly to all creatures. The *Kan-Ying-P'ien* condemns the pleasures of the chase as ignoble. Plants also it reckons as living things, and demands that no damage be unnecessarily done them. There is an edition of this collection of maxims in which each maxim that treats of compassion for animals is elucidated by a few anecdotes.

In the rules of the Taoist orders of monks, by which the monks are still bound today, kindness to living creatures is made a duty. For example, they are to avoid pouring boiling water on the ground because by so doing they might kill or hurt insects.

For Indian thought the principle of the unity of all existences — human, animal and vegetable — is a matter of course. It is a feature of the Brahmanic belief that all individual souls proceed from the Universal Soul (the Brahman) and return to it again. And it is also found in the doctrine of reincarnation. The relations of man to the animal creation are determined by the command- ment not to kill and not to harm, which is usually described as Ahimsa. The idea of Ahimsa is probably not of Brahmanic origin, for, if it were, it would be inexplicable that the Brahmins should continue the custom of animal sacrifice. It seems to have arisen among Jaina monks, and the beginnings of this order of monks probably go back to the eighth century B.C.

The origin of the Ahimsa commandment, strange as it may seem to us, was not a lively pity for the animal creation, but the idea of keeping pure from the world. The Ahimsa commandment derived from the general principle of non-activity as based on Indian world- and life-negation, and as the monks endeavored to realize it in renunciation of the world. It was an ethical interpreta- tion of this principle. But when once the commandment not to kill and not to harm had achieved recognition, it was inevitable that it should later be understood and expounded as having arisen from the motive of compassion. And this is what actually came about with Buddha (died circa 480 B.C.).

But Indian compassion for the animal creation is incomplete. It enjoins only that men shall refrain from killing and hurting living creatures, but not that these shall be actively assisted. Because it is so limited, we see that the conception of Ahimsa did not arise from a lively feeling of compassion, but was originally an ethical application of the principle of non-activity derived from world- and life-negation. Of course, in India, compassion does not remain strictly enclosed within the sphere of abstinence from action. But in so far as Indian ethics are under the domination of world- and life-negation, they are not in a position to demand as a principle active compassion for the animal creation.

The question is often propounded why sympathy with animals was not laid down as a Christian commandment, especially as the Jewish law already contained instructions for the care of animals. The explanation must be sought in the fact that primitive Christendom lived in the expectation of the speedy end of the world and therefore believed the day to be near when all creatures would be delivered from their sufferings. St. Paul speaks of the longing of the whole creation for early redemption in the eighth chapter (verses 18-24) of the Epistle to the Romans. His deep sympathy with the animal creation finds expression in those verses. But because the end of the natural world with its suffering and misery was believed to be so near, there was as little thought for the protection of animals as for the abolition of slavery. In this way we can understand how it is that the Christian commandment of love does not expressly demand sympathy with animals, although this idea is really implicit in it.

Every man and woman who thinks simply and naturally cannot do otherwise than express love in action, not only on behalf of human beings, but also on behalf of all living things. We, who no longer expect the redemption of the whole creation from suffering as the outcome of the immediate end of the world, are compelled by the commandment of love contained in our hearts and thoughts, and proclaimed by Jesus, to give rein to our natural sympathy for animals. We are also compelled to help them and spare them suffering as far as it is in our power.

So we Europeans and descendants of Europeans, in spite of the fact that the philosophic thought current among us did not lead us in any such direction, have reached a point where we turn our attention to the question of our relationship and our responsibility to the animal creation and place the demands of love for animals side by side with the demands of love for human beings.

We gladly admit that the question of man's relationship to the animals began to play a part in Chinese and Indian thought earlier than it did among us, and that Chinese and Indian ethics lay down as principles the duties and responsibilities of human beings towards the rest of creation. But at the same time we believe we can establish the fact that what we are doing today, by word and deed, to spread the feeling of responsibility towards animals also has its significance and is able to offer a stimulus to Chinese and Indian ethics.

For it is not as if Chinese and Indian ethics really solve the problem of the relationship of man to animals. What they have to offer in this regard is fragmentary and cannot satisfy us. What is great about Chinese ethics is that they stand for natural, active compassion for the animal creation. But they are far from elucidating the problem of man and the animal creation in all its implications. And they have failed to educate the people to true kindness toward animals. All too early, Chinese thought came to a standstill. It froze in scholasticism and clung only to what had been handed down by tradition from the thinkers of antiquity about love for living creatures instead of developing it further.

Indian ethics are unsatisfying in what they say about men and animals because they command only compassionate non-killing and non-harming but not compassionate helping. The difficult problem, whether man can avoid killing and harming, is neither propounded nor dealt with. Men are allowed to cherish the illusion that they can avoid killing and harming living creatures and really fulfill the Ahimsa commandment. Indian ethics neglect to teach men to feel the whole weighty burden of their responsibility toward animal creation.

Philosophy wants to imagine ethics as a well-ordered system of duties and commandments which can be well fulfilled. But as soon as we in any way recognize the principle of love, even if we limit it to human beings, we arrive actually at an ethic of boundless responsibilities and duties. Love cannot be put under a system of rules and regulations. It issues absolute commands. Each of us must decide for himself how far he can go towards carrying out the boundless commandment of love without surrendering his own existence and must decide, too, how much of his life and happiness he must sacrifice to the life and happiness of others.

Because the extension of the principle of love to the animal creation means so great a revolution for ethics, philosophy shrinks from taking this step. It would like to cling to a system of ethics which prescribes for man his behavior toward other men and toward society in clear, reasonable commandments without exaggerated demands.

Anyone who seriously studies the question of sympathy with animals knows that it is easy to preach such sympathy in general, but extraordinarily difficult to lay down rules for making it effective in individual cases. Not only does there come into consideration here the question of when the existence or the welfare of an animal may be sacrificed to the existence or the needs of man, but also the question of how we are to decide whether the life or well-being of one animal may be sacrificed to the life or well-being of another. How is it justifiable for us to catch insects to give them as food to preserve the life of a poor, helpless little bird which has lost its mother? By what principle do we decide to destroy a multitude of other lives so that we may preserve the one?

An ethic that tries to teach us reverence and love for all life must at the same time open our eyes in pitiless fashion to the fact that in manifold ways we find ourselves under the necessity of destroying and harming life, and that we are constantly engaged in grievous conflicts, if we have the courage not to let ourselves be stupefied by want of thought.

Because European philosophy has an instinctive feeling for the difficulties in which ethics finds itself if it proclaims the commandment of love for all living beings, it has endeavored right down to our time to rest on the principle that ethics is concerned only with the relations of man to his neighbor and to human society, and that love for the animal creation is only important in a certain measure as an addition to real ethics. It cannot, indeed, escape the notice of ethics that in this way it is setting itself in opposition to our natural feeling. But it would rather take this responsibility than resolve to engage in the difficult adventure of an ethic of boundless duties and boundless responsibilities.

But ethics is defending a position that is already lost. Thought cannot avoid the ethic of reverence and love for all life. It will abandon the old confined systems of ethics and be forced to recognize the ethics that knows no bounds. But on the other hand those who believe in love for all creation must realize clearly the difficulties involved in the problem of a boundless ethic and must be resolved not to veil from man the conflicts in which this ethic will involve him, but allow him really to experience them.

To think out in every implication the ethic of love for all creation — this is the difficult task which confronts our age.   [*Protection*]

16

An Absolute Ethic

What is the attitude of the ethics of reverence for life when confronted by the conflicts which arise between the inner compulsion toward self-sacrifice and the necessity for self-assertion?

I myself am subject to the division of the will-to-live within myself. In a thousand ways my existence is in conflict with others. The necessity of taking life and harming life is imposed upon me. When I walk along a lonely path my foot brings pain and death to the tiny forms of life that populate it. To preserve my life, I must defend it against the life that injures it. I become a persecutor of the little mouse that lives in my house, a murderer of the insect that wants to build its nest there, a mass-murderer of the bacteria that endanger my life. I get my food by the destruction of plants and animals. My happiness is built upon injury to my fellow creatures.

How can ethics be maintained in the light of the cruel necessity into which I am thrown by the inner conflict of the will-to-live?

The ordinary ethic tries to compromise. It seeks to show how much of my life and my happiness I must sacrifice, and how much I am permitted to preserve at the expense of the life and happiness of others. Out of these judgments it fashions an experimental, relative ethic. It sets forth as ethical what in reality is not ethical but rather a mixture of the ethical with non-ethical necessity. In this way monstrous confusion arises. Because of it the conception of the ethical is increasingly obscured.

The ethic of reverence for life recognizes no relative ethic. It considers good only the maintenance and furtherance of life. It brands as evil all that destroys and hurts life, no matter what the circumstances may be. It keeps no store of appropriate compromises between ethics and necessity ready for use. Again and again, and always in some original fashion, the absolute ethic of reverence for life brings a man to terms with reality. It does not rid him of conflicts, but it forces him to decide for himself in every case how far he can remain ethical, and how far he must yield to the necessity of destroying and harming life and suffer the ensuing guilt. A man does not make moral progress by being instructed in compromises between the ethical and the necessary, but only by hearing ever more clearly the voice of the ethical, by being ruled ever more strongly by a longing to preserve life and to promote it, and by withstanding ever more stubbornly the necessity for destroying and injuring it.

In ethical conflicts a man can make only subjective decisions. No one can decide for him in any case where the extreme limit of possibility lies in his persistence in preserving and promoting life. He alone can make this decision, being guided in it by a feeling of the most elevated responsibility toward other life.

We must never become callous. When we experience the conflicts ever more deeply we are living in truth. The quiet conscience is an invention of the devil.

What does reverence for life say about the relations between man and the animal world?

Whenever I injure any kind of life I must be quite certain that it is necessary. I must never go beyond the unavoidable, not even in apparently insignificant things. The farmer who has mowed down a thousand flowers in his meadow in order to feed his cows must be careful on his way home not to strike the head off a single flower by the side of the road in idle amusement, for he thereby infringes the law of life without being under the pressure of necessity.

Those who experiment upon animals by surgery and drugs, or inoculate them with diseases in order to be able to help mankind by the results obtained, should never quiet their consciences with the conviction that their cruel action may in general have a worthy purpose. In every single instance they must consider whether it is really necessary to demand of an animal this sacrifice for men. And they must take anxious care that the pain be mitigated as far as possible. How many outrages are committed in scientific institutions through the failure to administer anesthetics to save time and trouble! And how many others by subjecting animals to torture simply to demonstrate phenomena already generally known!

By the very fact that animals through these painful experiments have contributed so much of value to suffering mankind, a new and special bond of solidarity has been established between them and us. From this arises the obligation for each of us to do every possible good to all animals everywhere. Whenever I help an insect in its need I am only trying to discharge something of the ever-growing debt of mankind to the animal world. Whenever an animal is somehow forced into the service of men, every one of us must be concerned for any suffering it bears on that account. No one of us may permit any preventable pain to be inflicted, even though the responsibility for that pain is not ours. No one may appease his conscience by thinking that he would be interfering in something that does not concern him. No one may shut his eyes, and think that the pain, which is therefore not visible to him, is nonexistent. Let no one make the burden of his responsibility light. When so much mistreatment of animals continues, when the cries of thirsty beasts from our railway cars die out unheard, when so much brutality prevails in our slaughter houses, when animals meet a painful death in our kitchens from unskilled hands, when animals suffer incredibly from merciless men and are turned over to the cruel play of children, we all bear the guilt for it.

We are afraid of shocking people if we let it be noticed how much we are moved by the suffering man brings to animals. We think that others may have become more "rational" than we, and may accept as customary and as a matter of course the things we have gotten excited about. Once in a while, however, a word suddenly slips out which shows that even they have not yet become reconciled to this suffering. Now they come very close to us though they were formerly strangers. The masks with which we were deceiving each other fall off. Now we learn from each other that no one is able to escape the grip of the cruelty that flourishes ceaselessly around us.

The ethic of reverence for life prompts us to keep each other alert to what troubles us and to speak and act dauntlessly together in discharging the responsibility that we feel. It keeps us watching together for opportunities to bring some sort of help to animals in recompense for the great misery that men inflict upon them, and thus for a moment we escape from the incomprehensible horror of existence.   [*Kultur,* pp. 247-251]

Biographical Data

(Compiled from reminiscences shared with the editor during long and pleasant evenings in Dr. Schweitzer's study-office-bedroom at Lambarene, Gabon, French Equatorial Africa.)

January 14, 1875. Albert Louis Philipp Schweitzer was born at Kaysersberg, Haute Alsace. During this year his father became pastor at Gunsbach, in the Munster Valley, Haute Alsace.

1880–1884. In the village school.

Autumn 1884 to autumn 1885. *Realschule* at Munster.

Autumn 1885 to August 1893. *Gymnasium* at Mulhouse, Haute Alsace.

June 18, 1893. Passed his matriculation examination for the university at the Mulhouse *Gymnasium*.

October, 1893. First sojourn in Paris. Studied the organ under Widor.

November 1893 to spring 1898. Student at the University of Strassburg in theology, philosophy, and musical theory, living in the Theological Seminary of St. Thomas (Collegium Wilhelmitanum). While at the university wrote his first book, a small brochure in French upon the life and activity of Eugène Munch, his former organ teacher at Mulhouse, who died of typhoid fever at the beginning of his career — a book intended for the friends and pupils of this artist. The book was printed at Mulhouse in 1898.

April 1, 1894 to April 1, 1895. Military service in the 143d infantry regiment.

Autumn 1897. Wrote thesis required of all candidates for the first examination in theology upon the topic prescribed by the faculty: "The Idea of the Last Supper in Daniel Schleiermacher, Compared with the Ideas of Luther, Zwingli and Calvin." In studying Schleiermacher's idea of the Last Supper he was struck by the fact that Schleiermacher insisted that Jesus did not ask the disciples to repeat this meal, and that the disciples had done so of their own initiative.

May 6, 1898. Passed his first theological examination before the faculty. The examination consisted of four written papers on the New Testament, the Old Testament, Church History and Dogmatics; an oral examination in five parts, New Testament, Old Testament, Church History, Dogmatics and

Practical Theology; and a sermon preached in a church with two of the examiners present. As a result of this examination he received the Goll Scholarship, the recipient of which was pledged to take his licentiate in theology at Strassburg within six years or return the money received.

Summer 1898. Continued to study philosophy at the University of Strassburg under Ziegler and Windelband. At the end of the summer he proposed to Professor Ziegler as the theme of his doctoral thesis a study of Kant's philosophy of religion in relation to the different stages of what seemed to him its constant evolution. At this time he was not living at the Theological Seminary.

Autumn 1898 to spring 1899. Under the Goll Scholarship, studied at the Sorbonne in Paris, living at 20 Rue de la Sorbonne. He neglected the courses at the college, devoting himself to his organ studies under Widor, and to his thesis on Kant. He paid almost no attention to the books about Kant, confining his attention to a minute study of the text and the language peculiarities, in order to discover the different stages in the development of the thought of Kant which was in a state of constant flux.

March 12, 1899. Returned to Gunsbach and revised his manuscript.

April to July, 1899. Used the Goll Scholarship for further study of philosophy and organ at Berlin.

End of July, 1899. Returned to Strassburg for his examination in philosophy with Windelband and Ziegler. Received degree of Ph.D.

Autumn of 1899. Returned to his old room in the Collegium Wilhelmitanum (St. Thomas Foundation) as a paying guest.

December 1, 1899. Appointed *Lehrvikar* at St. Nicholas in Strassburg, in compliance with the rules requiring a student to serve in a church for a period between his first and second theological examinations. There were two aged pastors at the church: Gerold, who was the leader of the liberal party, and Knittel, in whom orthodoxy and pietism mingled. Schweitzer began to work on a thesis on the historical origin of the Last Supper, to submit in fulfillment of the requirements for the degree of licentiate in Theology which one had to have to become a Privatdozent. This study led him to new conceptions about Jesus' messianic consciousness and his idea of sacrifice. At the same time Schweitzer worked on another book, *Das Messianitäts- und Leidensgeheimnis Jesu* (The Secret of the Messiahship and Passion of Jesus).

End of December, 1899. *Der Religionsphilosophie Kants von der Kritik der reinen Vernunft bis zur Religion innerhalb der Grenzen der blossen Vernunft* (The Religious Philosophy of Kant from the "Critique of Pure Reason" to "Religion within the Bounds of Mere Reason"), published by J. C. B. Mohr (Tübingen), to whom Professor Holtzmann had recommended the book. Schweitzer received from the editor about 600 marks and the copies which he had to furnish to the faculty.

July 15, 1900.   Passed second theological examination before a commission of learned pastors among whom sat a member of the faculty. The subjects were the same as in the first examination except that more emphasis was placed on practical theology. Busy with his studies of the Last Supper and the messianic consciousness of Jesus, he had not taken the time to review his previous studies in the various fields of theology and barely passed the examination.

July 21, 1900.   Obtained the degree of licentiate in Theology with his study of the Last Supper. To obtain this degree he also had to pass a very difficult colloquium before a commission of the faculty. Schweitzer passed *magna cum laude*.

September 23, 1900.   Ordained at St. Nicholas as a regular curate.

May 1, 1901 to September 30, 1901.   Upon the death of Erichson, received provisional appointment as Principal of the Theological Seminary (Collegium Wilhelmitanum), until Gustav Anrich could assume the office.

1901.   *Das Abendmahl in zusammenhang mit dem Leben Jesu und der Geschichte des Urchristentums* (The Last Supper in Connection with the Life of Jesus and the History of Early Christianity), published by J. C. B. Mohr (Tübingen). Volume I: *Das Abendmahlsproblem auf Grund des wissenschaftlichen Forschung des 19. Jahrhunderts und der historischen Berichte* (The Problem of the Last Supper in the Light of Nineteenth-Century Scientific Research and of the Historical Documents). Volume II, *Das Messianitäts- und Leidensgeheimnis: Eine Skizze des Lebens Jesu,* was published in the United States by Dodd, Mead and Company (New York) as *The Mystery of the Kingdom of God;* and in England by A. & C. Black (London) in 1925.

1902.   Appointed *Privatdozent,* thanks to the influence of Professor Holtzmann, and gave his inaugural lectures before the faculty upon the structure and tendencies of the Fourth Gospel. There followed in the summer of this year his first regular course on the Pastoral Epistles.

October 1, 1903.   Received permanent appointment as Principal of the Theological Seminary, when Anrich was appointed Extraordinarius in Church History in succession to Ernst Lucius, who had suddenly died. Moved from the city to his official quarters on the Embankment of St. Thomas, using earlier student room for his study. Received stipend of 2400 marks.

January 14, 1905. Thirtieth birthday. Decided to devote the rest of his life to the natives of equatorial Africa as a doctor of medicine.

1905 *J. S. Bach, le musicien-poète* (J. S. Bach, the Musician-Poet) published by Costallat in Paris, and in 1908 by Breitkopf & Härtel in Leipzig. The German edition was not a translation of the French book, but an entirely new work. The first chapter had been written in Bayreuth in 1905. Published also in English under the title *J. S. Bach.*

October 13, 1905. Made known his decision to serve as a missionary doctor, and entered into discussion with the Paris Missionary Society.

October 1905. Resigned from the directorship of the Theological Seminary, resignation to take effect in the spring of 1906.

1905 to 1913. Studied as a medical student at the University of Strassburg.

Spring 1906. Went to live in the mansard story of the house occupied by Dr. Curtius, the president of the Superior Consistory, in the same block of buildings with the Theological Seminary. There were three small rooms and a kitchen.

1906. Published *Von Reimarus zu Wrede: Eine Geschichte der Leben-Jesu-Forschung* (From Reimarus to Wrede: A History of Research in the Life of Jesus), (J. C. B. Mohr, Tübingen). Reimarus had been the first to emphasize the eschatological in Jesus, and Wrede, who died in 1907, had tried to eliminate all eschatology and all messianic ideas from the thought world of Jesus. The English edition, under the title *The Quest of the Historical Jesus,* was published in London by A. & C. Black in 1910. In 1906 there also appeared the treatise, *Deutsche und französische Orgelbaukunst und Orgelkunst* (The Art of Organ-Building and Organ-Playing in Germany and France), published by Breitkopf & Härtel, in Leipzig.

1906 to 1912. In the very restricted leisure moments left by his medical studies, his services as curate at St. Nicholas, his concert tours, and a very heavy correspondence, he began his study of the Pauline ideas. He was trying to find out how Paul, beginning with primitive, eschatological Christianity, arrived at a mysticism of dying and being born again "in Jesus Christ," and how this eschatological mysticism prepared the way for the hellenization of Christianity in the mysticism of "being in the Logos." He hoped to be able to finish the book before his departure for Africa, but succeeded only in

completing the introduction — a history of the various inter-
pretations of the writings of St. Paul. The completion of his
work was delayed by three other tasks. Towards the end of
this period of medical study he prepared, in collaboration with
Widor, an edition of Bach's organ works. He was, secondly,
engaged in enlarging and completing the second edition of
his *Geschichte der Leben-Jesu-Forschung*. To do this he had
to go through a great many new books, and particularly to
study the whole question of the historical existence of Jesus,
which had been brought to the fore by Drews. Thirdly, he
was engaged in preparing his thesis for the degree of doctor
of medicine, a study of the books which dealt with the question of Jesus' mentality from a psychiatric point of view.
This book necessitated a profound study of psychiatric
questions, and completed his history of the written lives of
Jesus.

May 1909. Gave address to organ section of Third Congress, International Society of Music, in Vienna, and played major role
in formulating International Regulations for Organ Building
recommended by the organ section.

1911. His *Geschichte der paulinischen Forschung von der Reformation
bis auf die Gegenwart* (History of the Study of Paul from the
Reformation to the Present Time) was published by J. C. B.
Mohr at Tübingen. The English edition under the title of
Paul and His Interpreters was published by A. & C. Black in
London in 1912. This book bore the dedication "Der medi-
zinischen Fakultät der Universität Strassburg in tiefer Dank-
barkeit für die gewährte Gastfreundschaft."

Autumn 1911. Played the organ for Widor's Second Symphony for
Organ and Orchestra at the Festival of French Music at
Munich.

Autumn to December 1911. Passed his examination in medicine at
Strassburg, during a period of terrible exhaustion.

Spring 1912. Resigned his posts as a teacher in the university and as a
preacher at St. Nicholas. His last lectures were on the evalua-
tion of religion from the point of view of historical criticism
and the natural sciences.

June 18, 1912. Married Helene Marianne Bresslau, daughter of the
Strassburg historian. Afterwards retired to his father's house
in Gunsbach to work on the second edition of his *Geschichte
der Leben-Jesu-Forschung,* assisted by his wife.

February 1913. Having completed his year of internship, and having
finished his thesis, he received the degree of doctor of medicine.

March 26, 1913. Embarked at Bordeaux for Africa, where he established a hospital on the grounds of the Lambarene station of the Paris Missionary Society. The place was called Andende.

1913.   The second edition of his *Geschichte der Leben-Jesu-Forschung* was published by J. C. B. Mohr at Tübingen. In the same year J. C. B. Mohr published in Tübingen *Die Psychiatrische Beurteilung Jesu* (The Psychiatric Study of Jesus). The proofs of the former book were corrected on the train from Paris to Bordeaux, where Schweitzer was to embark for Africa. The proofs of the latter were corrected by a friend in Strassburg while Schweitzer was at sea. Six volumes in the edition of Bach's works were finished before his departure. The last three volumes of choral compositions were completed in Africa during the first few months after his arrival there, but for various reasons these volumes have not yet been published.

August 5 to end of November 1914.   Interned with his wife at Lambarene as an enemy alien. Began his work on *The Philosophy of Civilization,* about which he had been thinking since the summer of 1899, and which an editor in England had requested about 1910. This work was continued even after November, when he was allowed more liberty to continue his hospital work.

September 1915.   During a two-hundred-kilometer journey up the Ogowe River to N'Gomo, suddenly the words "Reverence for Life" came to him as the elementary and universal conception of ethics for which he had been seeking. Upon this principle his whole philosophy of civilization was subsequently based.

September 1917.   Transferred with his wife to France as a civil intern. At Garaison in the Pyrenees continued to work on his philosophy.

Spring 1918.   Transferred to St. Rémy de Provence. Served as a doctor during the daytime and worked on his philosophy during the evenings.

End of July 1918.   Returned to Alsace in an exchange of prisoners.

1919 to 1921.   Accepted a post as preacher at St. Nicholas, and also a post as physician in the City Hospital of Strassburg. Occupied the empty parsonage on the Nicholas Embankment through the courtesy of the Chapter of St. Thomas. Submitted to operation, from which he did not fully recover for two years.

January 14, 1919.   Daughter born on his birthday.

About Christmas 1919.   Received invitation to give course of lectures at Uppsala in Sweden.

After Easter 1920.   Delivered lectures on the Olaus-Petri Foundation at the University of Uppsala, using as his subject the problem of world- and life-affirmation and ethics in philosophy and world-religions, working up the material afresh, as he had left his manuscripts in Africa. Gave a series of organ concerts and lectures in Sweden to pay off the debts which he had incurred for the hospital.

Middle July 1920. Returned to Strassburg to write in a few weeks a book on his experiences in Africa, which the editor Lindblad at Uppsala had requested.

1920. Honorary doctorate in divinity from theological faculty in Zürich. The Swedish edition of *Zwischen Wasser und Urwald* (Between the Water and the Jungle) was published by Lindblad at Uppsala. The book was published in German in 1921 by by Paul Haupt at Berne, and in 1925 also by C. H. Beck in Munich. Published in English under the title *On the Edge of the Primeval Forest*.

Spring 1921. Played the organ at the Orféo Català in Barcelona for the first production of the St. Matthew Passion in Spain.

April 1921. Gave up both positions at Strassburg, depending thenceforth for his support on his pen and his organ. Returned to Gunsbach, where he was appointed vicar to his father, in order to work quietly on his *Philosophy of Civilization*. Retained a room in Strassburg on the rue de l'Ail (Knoblauchgasse).

Autumn 1921. In Switzerland.

November 1921. In Sweden.

January and February 1922. Courses of lectures in England at Mansfield College, Oxford, on Dale Foundation, and at the Selly-Oak Colleges, Birmingham, on "Christianity and the World-Religions," and at Cambridge on "The Meaning of Eschatology," and at the Society for the Science of Religion in London on "The Pauline Problem." Also gave a series of organ concerts in England.

Spring 1922. Three more weeks of lectures and concerts in Sweden, followed by lectures and concerts in Switzerland.

Summer 1922. Working undisturbed on *The Philosophy of Civilization*.

Autumn 1922. More lectures and concerts in Switzerland, a series of lectures in Copenhagen on the invitation of the theological faculty, followed by lectures and concerts in various Danish cities.

January 1923. Spoke in Prague on "The Philosophy of Civilization."

Spring 1923. *The Philosophy of Civilization* published by C. H. Beck in Munich and Paul Haupt in Berne in 1923 in two volumes, *The Decay and Restoration of Civilization,* and *Civilization and Ethics.* Also in the same year Allen and Unwin published in London *Christianity and the World-Religions*. The German edition appeared in 1924 with Paul Haupt in Berne.

February 1924.   Wrote *Memoirs of Childhood and Youth*. The English edition was published by Allen and Unwin in London the same year.

February 14, 1924.   Left Strassburg for Africa, leaving his wife behind in Europe because of her poor health. Carried with him preliminary drafts of his book on *The Mysticism of Paul the Apostle* on which he had been working during all the years of his first sojourn in Africa and during his sojourn in Europe from 1917 to 1924.

April 19, 1924 to July 21, 1927.   Second sojourn in Africa. Compelled to reconstruct the hospital, which had fallen into ruin, and later to transfer it to a new and roomier site at Adolinanongo, where the new buildings were constructed of hardwood and corrugated iron. During this period of rebuilding he was compelled to abandon all literary work. In the morning he worked as a doctor, in the afternoon as a laborer. The number of patients constantly increased and he was obliged to send to Europe for two more doctors and two more nurses. Just as he was about to resume work on *The Mysticism of Paul the Apostle,* a severe famine and an epidemic of dysentery set in, and again his writing had to be abandoned. He was able, however, to keep up his regular practice on his piano with organ pedals. Reports of his work in Africa were sent to Europe in the form of letters to friends and supporters and published in three small volumes, under the title *Mitteilungen aus Lambarene* (Reports from Lambarene), by C. H. Beck in Munich and Paul Haupt in Berne. The first, covering the period from spring to autumn 1924, appeared in 1925; the second, covering the period from autumn 1924 to autumn 1925, appeared in 1926; and the third, covering the period from autumn 1925 to summer 1927, appeared in 1928.

1925.   Received honorary degree of Doctor of Philosophy from University of Prague *in absentia.*

July 1927 to December 1929.   In Europe. Lectures and concert tours in Sweden, Denmark, Holland, Germany, Switzerland, England, and Czechoslovakia. During this period devoted all his spare time to his book on *The Mysticism of Paul the Apostle*. A large part of this book was written in Königsfeld in the Black Forest, where he had established a summer home. The book was finished on the boat which took him back to Africa.

August 28, 1928.   Received Goethe Prize from the City of Frankfort, delivering an address there on his indebtedness to Goethe.

This was the second time that this prize had been awarded, Stephan George having been the first to receive it. With the money he received he built a home in Gunsbach where he planned also to house the personnel of his hospital during their vacations in Europe. Schweitzer's address on Goethe was published by Henry Holt in New York in 1929, following the text published in the *Hibbert Journal* in July of the same year.

December 26, 1929 to January 7, 1932.   Third sojourn in Africa. During this sojourn he wrote his autobiography. In 1929 he had written for the editor Felix Meiner (Leipzig) a brief autobiographical sketch for the seventh volume of his *Philosophie der Gegenwart in Selbstdarstellungen* (Present-Day Philosophy in Self-Portraits). This particular chapter was republished by the editor as a small book, but as Schweitzer thought that readers might consider this a real autobiography and draw false conclusions from it, he decided to enlarge it to include a review of his life and his literary works. The book appeared in German under the title *Aus meinem Leben und Denken,* published by Felix Meiner in Leipzig in 1931, and the following year it was published in England under the title *Out of My Life and Thought.* Upon the completion of the autobiography, Schweitzer continued his work on the third volume of his *Philosophy of Civilization.* This work in turn was interrupted by an invitation received in October 1931, from the burgomaster of Frankfort to deliver a memorial address on the anniversary of the death of Goethe. The acceptance of this invitation necessitated an earlier return to Europe than he had contemplated. The first draft of the address was prepared at Lambarene towards the close of 1931 and the address was completed on the steamer that took him to Europe in January 1932.

1931.   *More from the Primeval Forest* was published in England by A. & C. Black. This was a translation of the German book *Das Urwaldspital zu Lambarene,* which had been published by Beck at Munich in 1931. This latter book in turn brought together into a single volume the three little books, *Mitteilungen aus Lambarene,* which had been published in 1925, 1926, and 1928. The American edition, published by Henry Holt and Company in New York, bore the title, *The Forest Hospital at Lambarene.* Received honorary degrees of Doctor of Divinity and Doctor of Music from University of Edinburgh *in absentia.*

February 1932 to April 1933.   In Europe. Lectures and concerts in Holland, England, Sweden, Germany and Switzerland.

Worked on the third volume of *The Philosophy of Civiliza-tion,* completing the plan for the whole book and sketching out the different chapters.

March 22, 1932.   Memorial address in Frankfort on 100th anniversary of death of Goethe. The address was published in the same year by C. H. Beck in Munich.

June 12, 1932.   Received honorary degree of Doctor of Divinity from University of Oxford.

June 27, 1932.   Received honorary degree of LL.D. from St. Andrews University.

April 21, 1933 to January 11, 1934.   Fourth sojourn in Africa. All of his leisure was employed upon the third volume of his philosophy, and in preparation of the Gifford Lectures which were to be given in 1934 and 1935.

February 1934 to February 1935.   In Europe. The spring and summer were spent upon the third volume and upon the preparation of the Gifford Lectures.

Autumn 1934.   Hibbert Lectures at Manchester College, Oxford, under the subject "Religion in Modern Civilization." These lectures were later repeated at London University College. They have not yet been published, but a fairly adequate summary of them was printed in *The Christian Century* in November 1934.

November 1934.   Gifford Lectures at Edinburgh, in which he en-deavored to trace the progress of human thought from the great thinkers of India, China, Greece, and Persia. The chapter upon the evolution of Indian thought grew to such an extent that he decided to publish it as a separate book. It was issued under the German title of *Die Weltanschauung der indischen Denker* (The World View of the Indian Thinkers) by Beck at Munich in 1934; under the French title *Les Grands penseurs de l'Inde* (The Great Indian Thinkers) by Payot at Paris in 1936; and under the English title *Indian Thought and Its Development* by Hodder and Stoughton at London in 1936. The same year it was published by Henry Holt and Company in New York.

February 26, 1935 to August 22, 1935.   Fifth sojourn in Africa. This stay was terminated by his obligation to return to Europe for the second series of Gifford Lectures, which were largely written in Africa.

September 1935 to February 1937.   In Europe.

November 1935.   Second course of Gifford Lectures. Lectures and concerts in England.

1936.   Working on his philosophy, translating into French his book *Les Grands penseurs de l'Inde,* and in October making records of organ music for Columbia Records in London upon the organ of St. Aurelia's at Strassburg.

February 18, 1937 to January 10, 1939. Sixth sojourn in Africa. He carried with him the manuscript for his philosophy, believing that now at last he would be able to finish it, but the increasing responsibilities of the hospital left him little leisure. For some time he thought that the extent of the material would make it necessary to publish two volumes instead of one. He could not bring himself to this decision, however, and finally set to work to compress his thought into the compass of a single book. In order to simplify the problem he then planned to publish separately the chapters on the Chinese thinkers in whom he had become deeply interested.

1938. Wrote *From My African Notebook,* a little volume of anecdotes upon the ideas and the lives of the natives. Meiner of Leipzig published it under the title of *Afrikanische Geschichten* (African Stories) in 1938; Payot in Paris issued the French edition in 1941; Allen and Unwin in London issued the English edition in 1938.

January 10, 1939. Left for Europe with the hope of completing his third volume.

February 1939. Arrived in Europe, only to decide that war could not be avoided, and might break out at any moment. Decided, therefore, to return immediately to Africa.

February 12, 1939. Embarked again for Africa.

March 3, 1939 to October 1948. Seventh sojourn in Africa. During the first two years of the war he was able to work continuously on his book, but afterwards the scarcity of white personnel at the hospital made it necessary for him to devote himself almost exclusively to the care of the sick and to other hospital duties. Toward the end of 1945 he wrote an account of the war years at Lambarene, which was published in 1946 in Switzerland, Alsace, England and America, under the title *Lambarene 1939–1945.* The close of the war brought little relief, and it was not until 1947 that a rather more adequate personnel became available. Dr. Schweitzer then began to plan for his long-delayed return to Europe, but his departure from Africa did not take place until the fall of 1948. Just before his departure he wrote a little summary of the history of the hospital, which was published in Switzerland with photographs by Dr. Wildikann, one of the women who had spent some years with him in Africa, under the title *Das Spital im Urwald* (The Hospital in the Primeval Forest).

October 1948 to October 1949. Mostly in Europe with his wife at Königsfeld in the Black Forest, and at his home in Gunsbach, Alsace. During this sojourn in Europe he saw his four grandchildren for the first time in Switzerland. Working on a theological book and on the third volume of his *Philosophy of Civilization.* Made his first visit to America to give the principal address on Goethe for the Goethe Foundation at Aspen, Colorado, in July 1949, visiting New York, Chicago and Boston. Received honorary degree of LL.D. from the University of Chicago, June 11, 1949. Returned to Africa in October 1949.

October 1949 to May 1951. Eighth sojourn in Africa. Intensified his work for those afflicted with leprosy, using the discoveries of American medical science. Wrote a substantial epilogue, "The Conception of the Kingdom of God in the Transformation of Eschatology," for E. N. Mozley's book, *The Theology of Albert Schweitzer,* published by A. & C. Black, in London.

1950. Made a Chevalier of the Legion of Honor.

May 1951 to December 1951. In Europe. On September 16, 1951, received the 10,000-mark prize given by the West German Association of Book Publishers and Book Sellers at Frankfort, Germany, in recognition of his efforts in promoting world peace. The award was presented by Theodore Heuss, President of the West German Republic, an old-time friend of Schweitzer's. Schweitzer turned the money over to German refugees and destitute writers. Short visits to England, Holland, and Scandinavia.

December 3, 1951. Elected a member of the French Academy of Moral and Political Sciences.

December 1951 to July 1952. Ninth sojourn in Africa.

February 27, 1952. King Gustav Adolf awarded the Prince Charles Medal to Schweitzer for his great humanitarian achievements.

July 1952 to November 1952. In Europe. October 20, 1952, his formal reception into the French Academy of Moral and Political Sciences, succeeding Marshal Pétain. Spoke on "The Problem of Ethics in the Evolution of Human Thought."

November 1952 to May 1954. In Africa for tenth sojourn. Began to construct, in memory of his father and mother, a new village for Africans suffering from leprosy. This village is located about a half mile away from the main hospital and is of permanent construction with concrete foundations, hard wood timbers, raffia walls, and corrugated-iron roofs. It will accommodate about 250 patients.

October 30, 1953. The 1952 Nobel Peace Prize was awarded to Schweitzer *in absentia,* and was accepted in his name by the French Ambassador to Norway. Schweitzer announced that the money (roughly $36,000) would be used towards the expenses of constructing his leprosy hospital.

May 12, 1954. Was made a foreign honorary member of the American Academy of Arts and Sciences.

May 1954 to December 1954. In Europe. On November 4, 1954, at Oslo to deliver in the presence of King Gustav Adolf the long-awaited Nobel Peace Prize address on "The Problem of Peace in the World of Today."

December 1954 to May 1955. In Africa for his eleventh sojourn. Finished most of the work for the new leprosy hospital. On January 14, 1955, celebrated at Lambaréné his eightieth birthday. On that same day received the Gold Medal of the City of Paris.

May 1955 to December 1955. In Europe. On October 19, 1955, was made an honorary member of the British Order of Merit by Queen Elizabeth. (President Eisenhower is the only other honorary member.) On October 22, 1955, received an honorary degree of Doctor of Laws from the University of Cambridge. On November 11, 1955, President Heuss of the West German Republic awarded Schweitzer the order Pour le Mérite.

December 1955. Returned to Africa for his twelfth sojourn.

January 14, 1956, celebrated his eighty-first birthday in Lambaréné.

April 24, 1957. Published, under the auspices of the Nobel Prize Committee, a "Declaration of Conscience," appealing to the public opinion of the world to halt the testing of atomic weapons.

May 30, 1957. Death of Mme. Helene Schweitzer in Zurich.

May 30, 1957 to December 4, 1957. In Europe. Visited Switzerland and Germany.

December 1957. Returned to Africa for his thirteenth sojourn. Mme. Schweitzer's ashes buried outside his study-bedroom.

January 14, 1958. Celebrated his eighty-third birthday.

Index